About the Editor

RICHARD BALLANTINE's gift for sharing his cycling enthusiasms surfaced with RICHARD'S BICYCLE BOOK, published by Pan Books, which sold over a million copies, making it the best-selling bicycle book of all time. He founded *Bicycle Magazine,* launched the *Bicycle Buyer's Bible* and enjoys a large collection of bikes that ranges from antique high bikes to ultra-modern streamlined human-powered machines.

About the Author

JOHN SCHUBERT is one of America's most respected cycle journalists. Formerly executive editor of *Bicycle Guide Magazine* and editor of *Bicycling Magazine*, he has written numerous articles and tested hundreds of bikes during his career. He has toured and raced, and worked in a bicycle shop where he gained first-hand knowledge of bicycle maintenance. He is especially fond of tandem touring.

RICHARD'S
Cycling for Fitness

by John Schubert

Illustrations by
Peter Williams

Edited by
Richard Ballantine

Pan Books
London, Sydney and Auckland

Acknowledgements

It has been my privilege to work closely with hundreds of talented writers, athletes, medical professionals, engineers and fellow editors in cycling. Through these interactions, I came to understand cycling and have a clear vision of how to explain it to others.

I cannot remember every individual to whom I owe thanks, but I would like to try. For information on cadence and efficiency, Han Kroon; for information on aerodynamics and rider performance, aerodynamacists Jack Lambie, Chet Kyle and Peter Boor; rider position and bike fit, framebuilder Bill Boston and Fit Kit inventor Bill Farrell; foot position, shoe designer Dave Greenbaum and Biopedal inventors Erik Koski and Harry Hlavack; training, nutrition, and rider performance, Ed Burke, Fred Matheny, Peter Cavanaugh, David Costill, and Pat Ennis; biomechanics, Shimano's Shinpei Okajima; bike handling, Malcolm Boyd; race training and bike handling, Ed Wachter, Tom Prehn, coach Curt Bond and my club, the Lehigh Wheelmen; and on the psychological importance of ice cream, Arlene Plevin.

For aiding me in areas too numerous to mention, I must thank Crispin Mount Miller, John S. Allen, John Olsen, John Forester, Bernard Klees, Dr. David Smith, David Gordon Wilson, Gary Fisher, Frank Berto, Tom Walz and Imre Barsy.

Editor Richard Ballantine improved my work greatly, and that's not something writers say about editors very often.

Special thanks are due to my physical therapist, my first editor for this book, and my favourite tandeming companion, Anne M.K. Schubert. Without her, Ballantine's job would have been hopeless.

—John Schubert

First published 1989 in Great Britain by Oxford Illustrated Press

This edition published 1991 by Pan Books Ltd, Cavaye Place, London SW10 9PG

9 8 7 6 5 4 3 2 1

ISBN 0 330 31574 9

Printed in Great Britain by The Bath Press, Avon

Series created by Richard Grant and Richard Ballantine

Designed by Richard Grant

Produced by Tamshield Limited, London

**This book is dedicated to the
Schubert family tradition of
ascending Montana's Logan
Pass across the Continental
Divide**

Contents

Cycling —the Fitness Alternative

Sometime today, I'm going to walk away from my keyboard, hop on my bike, and go on my favourite ride. I'll buzz through three one-horse towns and arrive at a deserted road that meanders along a tree-shaded creek for several miles. I'll see some beautiful farms and country inns, my favourite waterfall, maybe some deer and raccoons if I'm lucky. Cool in summer, sheltered in winter, and beautiful year-round, that deserted road beckons me to come out and have fun.

Riding a bike is fun. It also happens to be good for you, but the big reason you do it is because it's fun. Riding well—swiftly, gracefully, powerfully, and with good endurance—is more fun. Fitness, health, and athletic achievement follow naturally.

Cycling is known as a sport that you can enjoy throughout your life. But it's more than that—it's many sports, which you can enjoy in entirely different ways—touring, racing, commuting and mountain biking. A good bike rider is one who can enjoy, and display the skills unique to, many different styles of riding.

If you're young and full of energy, you may think you'll always be racing your bike. Wait 20 years. Your life will change, your time to train will decrease, and you'll want to mellow out and enjoy the riding, and the riding companions that will be available to you then.

Similarly, if you're on in years and seeking to improve your health through cycling, you may surprise yourself. A year or two of pleasant outings may leave you so strong that you'll want to verify your newfound athletic prowess in a 100-mile century or a time trial.

And you may find yourself riding like a racer one week and like a tourist the next week. It's fun to be competitive and go fast, and it's also fun to sit back and sniff the flowers.

What do you dream of accomplishing through cycling? At the very least, a normal healthy person can dream of being a bike rider who is at optimum weight, with strong, strapping muscles, and who can effortlessly ride 40 or 50 miles at a clip. Hell, I've known heart attack patients and amputees who easily met these goals. You can, too. You can be the person who still has the energy to attack hills briskly and eagerly three or four hours into your ride.

If time and temperament permit, you may set much loftier goals. Would you like to tell

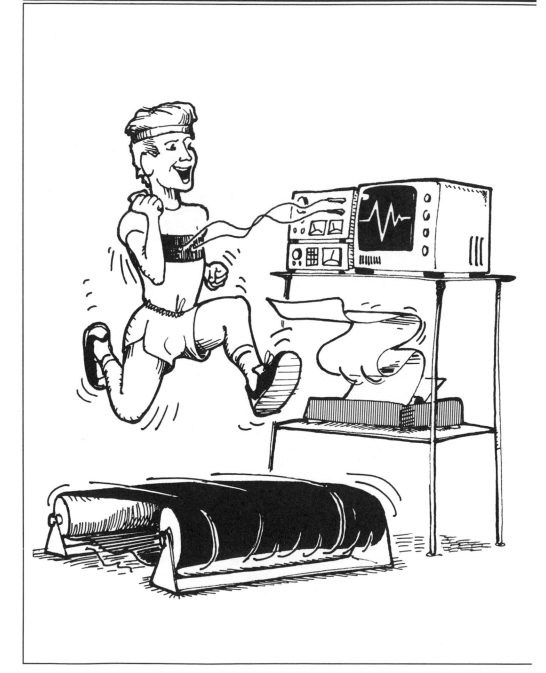

your friends you rode 100 miles in six hours (five on a flat course)? Or 25 miles in one hour? Or that you finished 200 miles in a one-day ride? Would you like to cover several counties in a day or really see the UK by riding from Land's End to John O'Groats.?

You can be swept up by the total immersion of racing in a peloton of 100 riders. You can enjoy cresting each new mountain and admiring the valleys below on a long tour. You

CAN EXERCISE DAMAGE YOUR HEALTH?

If you're 35 or over, and new to regular exercise, see your doctor and arrange a treadmill stress test (TST). This test usually consists of walking on a slow level treadmill while the electrical activity of the heart is continuously monitored. The speed of the treadmill is gradually increased until an intense work-out is accomplished. The purpose is not to see if you can beat the world, but to check that your heart rate is within bounds for your age and physical condition, and that there are no untoward problems or symptoms that could indicate a risk of having heart attacks.

According to Dr. Kenneth H. Cooper in *Running Without Fear,* for virtually all of us, including people with advanced coronary disease, the benefits of exercise far outweigh the slight risk of heart attacks or other tragedy during exercise. Of course, there's a right way and a wrong way to go about it. If you do have an increased risk of heart trouble, your exercise programme must be tailored accordingly. The specifics of your programme must be between you and your doctor, but to give you an idea, a typical high risk individual might ride gently for two to five hours per week. You can't win races that way, but you can enjoy most of the benefits and experiences outlined in this book.

Tragically, few people who need to tailor their exercise programme to their bodies actually bother. A recent Rhode Island study of 81 people who died during recreational exercise showed that 93 per cent had a medical history of heart disease or recognized risk factors--and yet only four of these people had undergone exercise testing.

Stress tests aren't cheap, but avoiding them is a false economy.

One last dour note: don't expect aerobic exercise to make up for unhealthy habits. Heart and blood circulation problems such as arteriosclerosis '. . . may develop quite independently of your exercise programme,' writes Cooper. 'Whatever your age, the disease is encouraged by risk factors such as smoking cigarettes, hypertension, high blood fats, diabetes, a family history of heart disease, or a high-stress life-style.'

In other words, don't come in from your bike ride and assume you can eat sticks of butter with impunity. Exercise doesn't make you immune to the effects of abuse.

can work together with friends to set personal best times for a 100-mile century. You can enjoy the perfection of crisp, precise control of your bike, like a graceful ballroom dancer or gymnast.

Sure, you'll get fit, and you'll have accomplishments to prove it. But perhaps best of all, every bike ride you take is a beautiful outing—fun!

Graceful Riding

Contents

Smooth Beats Strong

Most people become strong cyclists first, and only then, sometimes, graceful, flowing, smooth riders.

It is better to become a smooth cyclist first and a strong cyclist later. You'll enjoy the feeling of being one with the bike, the self-confidence that comes with knowing you're smooth and safe. You'll enjoy riding with your friends more because you can ride together as a group fluently, without getting in each other's way. Your group will move as one when you go around a corner, up or down a hill, or on rough road. You'll ride faster with less effort, so you can stay up with faster riders—and slower riders can stay up with you. You'll be far safer, negotiating potholes and heavy traffic with ease.

Pedalling

Graceful riding starts with pedalling smoothly, so you aren't fighting your own oscillations for control of the bike. A good rider can—and always does—spin his legs without any upper body motion. When he is standing, he minimizes upper body motion with a smooth style. (I used to practise this by riding a stationary exercise machine with a book balanced on my head. I could keep the book there for about 20 seconds while churning my legs at 95 rpm.)

Cyclists need to work at smooth technique, just as skiers and tennis players do. The bike's pedals define the path your feet follow, and the handlebars hold your hands in place, but oh how the in-between parts can flop around! And when the torso and arms twist back and forth, so does the front wheel: left with each right pedal stroke, and then vice versa.

Smooth riding is not difficult. The one mechanical requirement is correct saddle height, which is discussed in Chapter 4. Other than that, you just have to pay attention to isolating your upper body from your lower body's continuous movement. This is a learned skill that you should practise every time you ride. Stay seated, churn your legs, and make sure your torso is motionless. If you've never tried this before, you'll only be able to pedal smoothly at low cadences—say, 60 to 70 rpm. For a beginner, these speeds feel natural. You'll have to take it on faith that faster cadences will benefit you. But do try it, and force yourself to pedal briskly. Soon, you'll feel comfortable and smooth at higher cadences, and cruising at 90 or 95 rpm will feel natural.

Cadence

A brisk cadence is your best friend. This is something people sit around and argue about, but most good riders fan the pedals at pretty high speeds, cruising at 90 or 95 rpm. There are many compelling reasons to do so.

The biggest benefit is that your knees, which were designed before bicycles were invented, take less stress when you spin a low gear (turn the cranks quickly and easily) instead of pushing a high gear (turn the cranks slowly and with great effort). Many people have had to curtail or stop their riding because they buggered their knees by mashing big gears.

The second benefit is metabolic: you'll last longer and feel fresher if you can maintain a brisk cadence. The lower pedal effort which accompanies the combination of a lower gear rate and a faster cadence allows your muscles to work at well under their aerobic threshhold, and use the low octane fuels which your body has in unlimited supply—triglycerides and fatty acids. Higher muscle efforts, such as mashing big gears, use up precious stores of glucose—and when all your glucose is gone, you're ready to drop.

A novice cyclist, who has never ridden more than a couple miles at a time, rarely notices the loss of glucose until he's tired out. An experienced cyclist, however, is very picky about maintaining a brisk cadence, because he can feel the slight difference in his muscles. Excess effort eats up glycogen and produces lactic acid. As you learn to listen to your body, you'll become sensitive to the nuances of feelings that go with different levels of effort.

Some studies claim that slower cadences, such as 50 or 60 rpm, are more efficient than quicker cadences. These studies generally share three flaws.

One, the test subjects are non-cyclists who have never learned to pedal proficiently, and are apt to be better suited to a slower rhythm of movement. Even if the subjects are aerobically fit, they still don't know how to ride a bike—training effect is very specific to each sport.

Two, the exercise machines used do not closely mimic the pedalling conditions of a real bicycle. Poor saddle position, lack of toe clips and unnatural pedal resistance are common differences.

Three, and most importantly, slow cadences deliver the most energy to the pedals for the least oxygen consumed. But who said we had limited oxygen supplies? Cyclists are not scuba divers. Glycogen is our limited resource, and faster pedal cadences conserve that resource very well.

Remember, efficiency in the laboratory is not the same as efficiency on the road. Slow cadences are efficient for artificial, constant workloads, but not for the continually changing conditions of real cycling. Brisk cadences have always won races and kept tourists refreshed day after day.

Toe Clips

Toe clips and straps or shoe-cleat systems (such as Look, AeroLite or Cyclebinding) are essential if you're to pedal at quick cadences. Without a fastening method you'll have

WATCHING YOUR REVOLUTIONS

Do you know what 90 rpm feels like?

It's an extremely useful skill to have. When you're consciously aware of your cadence, you're more apt to maintain proper pace, and not lapse into a slow, slogging mode through inattention. Knowing what your proper cadence feels like makes it easier to anticipate your shifting needs, so you don't wait until you've lost valuable momentum before you shift.

The goal is to have a good feel for the correct general range—so you can keep your cadence somewhere in the 90s or know that you're sprinting at 115, but not so you can tell the difference between 95 and 97 rpm. The old-fashioned way to measure cadence is to count your pedal revolutions while keeping your eye on a stopwatch or sweep-second hand. Do this only on a quiet road. Count for 10 seconds and multiply by 6.

If you do this often enough, you'll develop a feel for cadences in your cruising range. In the extreme high-speed range of 120 rpm or above, this method is too difficult to use.

An alternative is to treat yourself to an electronic speedometer with a cadence function. Check specifications carefully; not all speedos have this feature.

trouble keeping your feet on the pedals. Beginners may wish to take a few rides without toe clips to get used to the bike, but your development as a bike rider will really take off when you start using toe clips.

You may have heard that toe clips allow you to pull up on the backside of the pedal stroke. Not so. Sure, you can do it for a few pedal strokes, to get up a short, steep hill, or for a brief sprint. But it's far too tiring to be useful for everyday pedalling. Good riders do exert a little upward muscle effort on the backside. However, many studies have shown that pulling only partially overcomes the rather substantial weight of the legs.

The main function of toe clips is to keep your feet on the pedals. Sounds undramatic, but without toe clips, you have to expend energy and attention to keep your feet from sliding off the pedals. Toe clips help save energy and cycling shoes with cleats aid this; I personally feel naked without cleats. With practice, you'll get familiar with cleats, and won't have any trouble getting your feet out of the pedals when you need to.

Steering

All that brisk pedalling will get smoother and smoother with practice, and it should be isolated from everything else you do—because you want to steer and brake smoothly, too. These and other skills must be practised, one at a time, in isolation, to be learned well. And you'll need to be pretty good at all of them to do fluent group riding, which is coming up later in this chapter.

How does a bicycle steer? A somewhat oversimplified explanation is: the bike is always off to one side of you, if only by 1/1000 inch. Left unchecked, it would move out from underneath you. You're always correcting this by steering the bike back into line. The trick to smooth riding is quite simple: make those steering corrections as small as possible. This is easy when you're going fast—the geometry of the bicycle gives it good self-stabilizing qualities at speed. When you're riding slowly it simply takes more mental attention to keep those corrections slight.

What happens when cornering? It depends on the rider. The inexperienced rider slows down more than necessary, overshoots the corner slightly, and needs to re-orient himself when he's finally settled on his new course. The experienced rider loses little momentum, leans naturally into the corner, follows a line selected in advance, and is heading at full speed in his new direction two pedal strokes after he's out of the corner.

That's enough to put 50 yards or more between two riders. What separates those riders? Experience and planning. The experienced rider knows how quickly he can get through the corner, and he doesn't slow down more than necessary. (After all, it takes work to speed up again!) He leans sharply into the corner, which allows him to keep up more speed and jump out of the corner and into his new heading in one fluid motion. The inexperienced rider is worried about bringing too much speed into the corner. He overshoots because he doesn't want to lean sharply. He may need to brake while in the corner, as he must choose between losing speed and increasing lean angle, and he'd rather lose speed. These ad hoc corrections and over-corrections play havoc with his path, so he has a bad line through the corner.

All this is a commercial for you to become comfortable with sharp lean angles. First of all, leaning is absolutely safe, unless you're on wet tarmac or loose gravel. Second of all, the sharper you lean, the quicker you can ride through a given corner. The laws of physics don't lie: you can corner ever faster with lean angles of up to 45 degrees. Not many of us are able to bank that steeply, although bike racers say that in the heat of competition, they lean much steeper than they'd ever dare in everyday training. You can pedal while leaning up to 28 degrees or so (the exact figure depends on your bike). That's pretty steep!

Practise smooth turns at slow speeds and extreme steering angles. Have contests with your friends to see who can make a U-turn in the narrowest space. The best such performance I've seen was by Bill McCready, owner of Santana Tandems. I was on the back of a three-seater captained by Bill as he U-turned its 92-inch wheelbase in ten feet. I can't do that, but at least I can U-turn an ordinary bike in a parking space, or U-turn a tandem on a narrow two-lane road. It's a handy skill; having practised it, allows me to pull it off the shelf and use it whenever I need to.

Braking

When I ride with intermediate level riders, I find that braking is the skill they're most likely to be behind in. They may be strong and smooth in other ways, but their use of brakes will be awkward and tentative. If we need to slow down for a bump or intersection, they'll tend to slow down more than necessary. Again, this handling deficiency can produce a 50-yard split without the quicker rider even trying.

What do you need to use your brakes well? First and foremost, you should be fluent in the emergency braking skills described in the sidebar on page 25. These are an extreme version of the technique you use every time you approach an intersection. (Of course, we're assuming your brakes and rims are in excellent mechanical condition. Many riders forget to lubricate their cables. After a year or two, this makes it very difficult to get good brake modulation.)

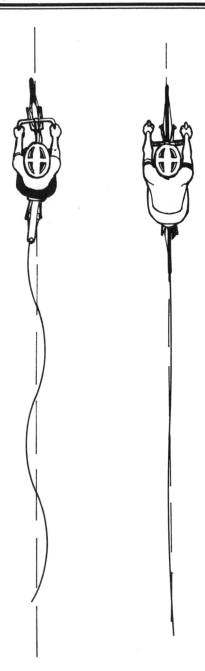

A bike is always moving from out-of-balance to in-balance to out-of-balance. The trick to riding in a smooth, straight line is to keep the steering corrections as small as possible.

Normally, you use both brakes simultaneously. When travelling in a straight line the more effective front brake is applied harder than the rear brake. Sometimes, though, only the rear brake should be used—for example, if you're cornering on a wet or loosely surfaced road. In these conditions using the front brake will encourage the front wheel to lose traction. Should braking and/or turning force cause the front wheel to skid, (something that doesn't happen on a dry surface, which is why we have pitch over accidents), the bike will understeer. It will follow its momentum instead of its front wheel.

Bumps

Another skill that separates intermediate from advanced riders is the ability to roll briskly over bumpy roads. I'm not talking about extreme stuff—I slow down for bridges of the wooden-plank or slick wet steel grating type as much as anyone—but about the usual bumps, tiny potholes, cracked surfaces, and undulations which all cyclists have to endure at some time.

When you're riding alone, you can always go around small bumps. But traffic, or the pressure of staying in formation with other riders, may force you to roll over these bumps. To do so, lift yourself out of the saddle and use your arms and legs as your springs and shock absorbers. Let the bike bob over bumps underneath you.

Learn to jump your bike. Whenever a big nasty pothole approaches, pull your body up

Sink down and compress. Jump up strongly.

abruptly, then pull on your handlebars and toe clips to lift the bike underneath you. This skill, too, takes frequent practice—otherwise, you'll have an abrupt landing, or aim poorly and land with a wheel in the pothole. A good way to hone accuracy is to stage a car park competition with friends and try jumping an old, small milk crate and offering small prizes for clearing the crate.

The best road racers on the Continent can jump their bikes sideways and upwards onto a kerb—while maintaining formation in the peloton. A trick worth knowing!

Looking Behind

You have to be able to look behind you when riding. For practice, have a friend ride behind you and count the number of fingers he holds up. This little exercise develops the ability to look behind quite quickly. Make sure you don't steer the bike in the direction you're looking. A helpful trick to keep the bike going straight: drop your left hand from the bars when you look over your left shoulder.

A rear view mirror does not save you from the need to look behind. For one thing, every rear view mirror has a blind spot. For another, looking behind you is an important kind of signal to other road users. Finally, some cyclists fixate on a rear view mirror at the expense of paying attention to the road ahead. These reservations noted, however, rear view mirrors can be quite handy.

Pull up bike by handlebars and toe clips. Land on rear wheel.

Approach kerbs and railway tracks head on; if you approach at an angle the front wheel will wash out and you'll spill.

Riding Dirt

Committed road riders need another skill: riding on dirt. There will be times when you face a gravel road, or tarmac so loose it might as well be gravel. There's little to worry about. The bike will bump and jostle underneath you more than on a decent surface, that's all. It won't jump out from underneath you. Being comfortable on dirt is essential. There will be times when you're forced to leave the road abruptly due to a fellow rider's error, a juggernaut or other imperfections in the world. If you're tight and scared, you may not handle the situation well. If you're smooth and loose, ready to jump that little culvert and then roll through on the weeds beyond it, you'll be far better off.

Anticipate road hazards. Sewer grates are slippery when wet, and some of them are designed to swallow your front wheel. Train tracks are nasty; you need to cross them at a right angle so they don't steer your front wheel out from underneath you. The same goes for small sideways ledges in the road surface, seams between concrete slabs, etc. All too many people injure themselves by riding over, or into, these obstacles at shallow angles. If you have to ride up a lip from a shoulder to a roadway, turn your front wheel abruptly and cross the lip at a sharp angle. Be conscientious: most bike riders know these principles in the abstract, but forget to stay alert and practise them on the road.

Gearing

The last skill in your bike handling repertoire is being at one with your derailleurs and gearing. No other subject causes so much controversy. I know riders who refuse to talk about gearing, fearing that they'll be branded as ignoramuses, and other riders who go a bit overboard, mapping out gearing programmes on their home computers and charts on logarithmic graph paper. I'd like to strike a middle ground. No computer programmes, or charts, and we won't talk endlessly about tinkering with sprockets. But you need to know how to make the hardware work for you.

Gearing is important because a finely developed cyclist is choosy about cadence. For a given ground speed, you're best off with whatever gear gives you a brisk cadence in the 90s. Much slower than that, and you are in a zone of high forces on a slowly moving knee joint, which spells trouble. Much faster, and the muscles generate lactic acid faster than blood circulation can wash it away—which hurts. So you need to shift gears frequently, to stay as close as possible to your optimum cadence and pedal pressure.

Hills and winds can make this an unending task. Suppose you're zipping along at 22 mph on flat ground. The road turns and ascends a one per cent gradient, then a two per cent gradient. Those inclines are so slight you're apt to ignore them visually. Yet, few riders are strong enough to bully over them by increasing work effort and maintaining the gear and cadence. With an equal work effort up the one per cent gradient, you'll slow down to 19 mph; up the two per cent gradient, $16^1/_2$ mph. Those are speed reductions of 14 and 25 respectively. So even these slight gradients demand a downshift to keep your cadence in the green zone.

The traditional racing bike and its lower priced spin-offs (formerly called the club racer, and now the triathlon bike or sport bike) are easy to shift in such a situation. Most of these bikes have freewheels which give you about a 15 per cent change in gear ratio from one cog to the next. All you have to do is move the shift lever enough to get the next cog over. When you reach a big hill, you shift the front derailleur, which buys you about a 20 per cent change in gear ratio.

Shifting a racing bike sounds simple, but some people don't bother. Many of the freewheels returned to bike shops for replacement have a completely worn out smallest (high gear) cog, some wear on the largest (low gear) cog, while the original factory grease is still hardly disturbed on the middle three or four cogs. These riders either spin like a hummingbird or slog like a pig in treacle. They don't maintain the sensible middle ground.

You, sir or madam, must put lots of wear on the middle cogs. Make a point of noticing small changes in terrain, in your effort level, in your cadence. Practise shifting one cog at a time. This has to be second nature, because poor shifting bogs you down needlessly.

The traditional touring bike and the mountain bike have three chainrings instead of two, and with good reason: steep hills and/or day-long fatigue demand lower gears for comfortable climbing. On steep trails, a mountain bike rider simply can't move without the third, small chainring, which is often called a bulldog, or granny gear.

Mountain bikes generally have the bulldog chainring added onto a setup something like that of a racing bike. Shifting is simple. But the customary gearing on most touring bikes differs, and is shifted differently. The freewheel is wide-range, with about a 20 per cent jump between cogs. The top two chainrings are only four or five teeth apart, giving about a 10 per cent jump. To get your next higher or next lower gear, you shift both the front and rear derailleurs. In exchange for having to make double shifts, you get more finely spaced gears—10 per cent jumps instead of 15, in round numbers. The arrangement is known as

BLAME IT ON THE HIGH-WHEELERS

Do you hate gear inches? Some bike riders—the non-mathematical types—wish gear inches had never been invented. Others dote on them to excess. Still others find them a useful tool.

Bicycle gearing is expressed in a fashion that dates back to the high-wheel bikes that were sold by wheel diameter. A bike with a 50-inch wheel went farther for each pedal stroke than a bike with a 45-inch wheel. When the safety bicycle was invented, with its two small wheels and chain, the nomenclature stuck. A bike with a 25-inch wheel diameter and a 2:1 drive ratio performed like the 50-inch ordinary. That's what you'd expect, multiplying the wheel diameter by the drive ratio. So they said it had 50 gear inches. A modern-day example: a bike with a 52-tooth chainring and a 17-tooth freewheel cog (52 divided by 17 gives 3.06) and a 27-inch rear wheel has a 83-inch gear (27 times 3.06 equals 83).

The lowest you can gear a bike with standard hardware is 20 inches. That will allow an unconditioned rider to climb steep hills at a comfortable 4 mph, without excess effort, and without having to get off and push. Touring cyclists love gears in this range for hauling their panniers up long gradients. Most touring bikes and mountain bikes have their lowest gear between 20 and 30 inches.

Gears between 30 and 40 inches climb steep hills easily.

Gears between 40 and 50 inches are for medium gradients, or steep gradients with a bit of effort. Today's sport riding bikes usually have their lowest gear in this range.

Gears from 50 to 60 are for moderate gradients; 60 to 70, slight gradients. Gears from 70 to 80 are for flat ground, 80 to 90, hard riding on flat ground, 90 to 100, downhill, above 100, down steep hills at high speeds.

'half step plus Granny' and it's a nice setup.

A bike designed for touring or mountain biking and equipped with low gears may be just the thing for your own personal fitness regimen. Steep hills, heavy riders, limited aerobic capacity, tender knees, or any combination of the above is cause to go for a bulldog gear. And if your doctor tells you to take it easy and you ride in hills, a bulldog gear is mandatory.

Motorists

Once you're in control of your bike's many functions, it becomes far easier to interact smoothly with other road users—most of whom are motorists.

Don't feel inferior to motorists. The roads are for you, too. The Highway Code gives you the rights and responsibilities of any vehicle.

I often hear bike riders complain that motorists are out to get them. With rare exceptions, this is untrue. Motorists are out to get somewhere. They don't care about cyclists one way or the other, and they won't as long as you make it easy for them to deal with your presence on the road.

You can greatly influence the behaviour of other road users in a way that benefits them and you. You do this by signalling, and that does not necessarily mean waving your hands. Everything you do on the bike is visible to motorists, and so even your body language is an implied signal. Once you discover this, it completely changes your attitude towards riding.

Generally, motorists respect a self-assured road user, and are impatient with tentative, unsure road users. That's how they react to other motorists, and that's how they react to you. Here's a specific example: I frequently see young bike riders on a road near where I live, riding slowly and wobbling a lot, constantly looking behind them for overtaking traffic. There's no shoulder for refuge. Over-

BRAKES AND THE ART OF STOPPING

A dog runs across your path at the bottom of your favourite descent. Can you stop as short as the laws of physics allow?

Many riders believe the key lies in buying the latest brakes with fancy price tags. Not so. Nice new brakes do feel great, and they make short stops slightly easier. However, a skilled rider can make an equally short stop on any bike with reasonable quality brakes in good condition.

Here's the key: the front brake has all the stopping power; the rear brake's contribution is incidental. You need to use all that stopping power without squeezing too hard and initiating a pitchover. A warning device that tells you when you're approaching pitchover is the rear wheel.

When you brake, weight comes off the rear wheel and transfers to the front wheel. If you hold your rear brake with moderate force and your front brake firmly, and your rear wheel starts to skid, that's a sign that you've lost just about all weight on the rear wheel. When that happens, it's time to let up on the front brake and transfer some weight back to the rear wheel.

Practise this technique routinely, every time you ride (when no other riders are behind you!). At first, you won't want to squeeze the front brake hard enough to get a rear wheel skid. That's okay. Get plenty of experience of the bike's feel at this corner of its performance envelope. One day you'll squeeze until you get a rear wheel skid, then calmly let up on the front brake. Once you've mastered this, you'll be a safer rider.

You can stop still shorter by sliding your rump backwards off the saddle until your outstretched arms just reach the brake levers.

taking motorists often do not give these riders the rather wide berth they need. So they head for the weeds every time a car overtakes them, and I'm sure they believe they need to do so.

I've ridden hundreds of times on the same road, and my experience is quite different. I maintain a smooth, steady path, with no visible steering wobble (at least, I hope none is visible!). I usually ride faster than these other people, but not always—I get tired, too. Even then, I make a point of carving a straight path. And motorists always give me an adequate berth when they overtake.

The young rider, when he looks around, is asking for permission to get in the motorist's way and delay him. The motorist denies that permission by maintaining his speed and course.

I don't ask. Instead, I maintain my course and show the motorist exactly what to expect from me. It takes the motorist very little effort to get around me. We both get to go our own ways, without disturbing each other. I glance behind whenever I hear an engine, but I don't make a big deal about it.

In your own riding, you've probably discovered this same effect. You may be able to use it more than you now do, because it carries over into manoeuvres other than routine overtaking. It can expedite your turns, lane changes, and position-in-lane changes. Learn the appropriate signals and these manoeuvres become much easier.

The next important consideration after maintaining a certain course is your position in the lane. If you track close to the gutter, you encourage motorists to zoom by you with scant clearance—and they will. At the same time, you give yourself inadequate space. A bike needs a reasonably wide path for safety. Remember, the road belongs to you as much as it belongs to anyone. If you very matter-of-factly claim the space you need, the average motorist won't challenge you, and he won't be delayed trying to get around you either. It's that tentative begging for permission that creates a problem.

There may be times when you need to assert yourself in this respect. For example, when riding in the countryside where the road often dips away on to a hard shoulder you may come under pressure from some motorists who wonder why you are not riding on the hard shoulder. Unless it's a designated cycleway let them wonder. Once they've passed you, it won't be a big issue in their lives.

Sometimes you need to change lanes or make a right turn. Done properly, these changes are also easy for other road users to deal with. You can get into position for a right turn, riding next to the road's centreline, and motorists will cruise by your left—going on their way and maintaining their indifference to you.

The first step in making a lane change is to look behind. You survey the scenery and, simply by looking, signal your intention to other road users. If there's a motorist behind you and you'd like to merge in front of him (we assume you're taking his speed and distance into account, and merging only if it's prudent), look straight at him and make a straight arm signal. Usually, the motorist will ease off and leave space for you. Quickly return your hand to the bars, your gaze forward, and crisply execute the lane change. If possible, display another arm signal before you start the turn.

Occasionally, you'll have to abort the merge right before you start. The motorist behind you will speed up and keep you from beginning your manoeuvre. Better to know early on!

Keep away from the gutter. Sometimes it even has sharks.

You can merge into position behind him and think about the rotten day he must have had at the office.

When riding on the right side of the lane in preparation for a right turn, you want people to know why you're there. Otherwise, someone will try to overtake you on the right. Your lane position, the right arm signal, and an especially smooth style will usually get your point across. If necessary (and it almost never is), use your left hand to usher overtaking motorists to pass on your left.

Sometimes you have to do a motorist's thinking for him. If he starts to overtake on a blind curve on a narrow road, move into the middle of the lane and extend your right arm downward, palm facing behind, in the standard slow/stop signal. When a lorry shows up halfway round the curve he'll thank you when he realizes you saved him from a head-on collision.

Common courtesy makes everyone's day more pleasant. Give other road users a break. Let the lorry pass, rather than making it come to a stop at the bottom of a steep hill. Make helpful gestures, ushering others on their way. And when someone makes a mistake, don't compound it by getting angry. Don't flatter yourself by thinking he was out to get you. Evade his error and go on your way.

When you're riding in groups, there are many special traffic-related considerations, discussed below. One reigns paramount: be picky about who you ride with. Don't ride with people who give out the wrong signals.

Group Riding

The minutiae of technique—brakes, gears, signalling turns—may seem like tiresome detail, but the reward is how they enhance your ability to ride in a group. All riders can enjoy riding together, regardless of their skill level, but it's well worth learning to ride in formation like racers do in training. It matters not whether you intend to race or not. Why? Because once you've learned formation, you won't want to ride any other way.

Riding in formation keeps riders together who would otherwise be separated by difference in ability. I frequently ride with companions much fitter than myself, and also with companions much less fit. What makes it possible for us to ride together is the great equalizer, drafting. The fitter rider spends most of the time at the front, forging a wind-break (and a one-third savings in energy expenditure) for the following rider.

Drafting allows us to go for mile after mile staying within two feet of each other. It's extremely rare that we separate by more than five or ten feet. Sometimes we'll cheat on hills, the more fit rider blasting ahead briefly, but at the top we promptly regroup.

Is this a grim, nose-to-the-grindstone tongue-hanging-out workout? No. When we feel like riding hard, we ride hard. But often we abandon drafting formation to ride side by side. We ride close enough to bump elbows, and we can converse without raising our voices. My riding companions—some active racers, some retired racers, some people who would never go near a bike race—have practised these riding skills so this kind of formation is what they prefer. We can talk, we never have to wait for each other, we can go fast, and we enjoy each other's company. We enter and exit every corner in formation, without losing any time. It feels neat.

What if you're a triathlete or biathlete, and drafting is forbidden in your races? Learn how anyway. It will make your training rides much more fun, increase the training benefit, and you'll enjoy the expertise. The bike handling practice is good for everyone.

How do you become comfortable riding at close quarters? Practise. The unskilled rider needs lots of space, because he can't control his vehicle precisely. That's why I harp on simple braking and steering. You need to master them before you learn to co-ordinate yourself with other riders.

This co-ordination begins with an understanding of the responsibilities you and your riding companions have when you ride in formation.

Drafting saves about one-third of the following rider's energy. What's less well-known is that it also saves a tiny amount—say, five per cent—of the lead rider's energy, the result of the way air closes in behind. Because the following rider benefits so much, he can cruise considerably faster than he's used to riding.

But he does so under very demanding conditions. Suppose you are in the lead. The following rider is inches from your rear wheel, and can't see the road directly ahead. He has

Wind envelopes. Drafting saves about one-third of the following rider's energy.

SAFETY IN NUMBERS

I was 35 miles into a century when I met this rider. Happy, energetic, obviously well-trained for the century, he was a disaster waiting to happen.

Why? He had an attitude I see all too often: because he was out with a few other riders, he ignored the rules of the road. He would go to the front of our small group, take strong, energetic pulls, and then swing off. Trouble was, when he swung off, he swung clear over to the right-hand side of the road. I vividly recall him swinging into the oncoming lane on a short, steep blind rise, where visibility was only about 20 yards. Had an oncoming car appeared, he would have been smashed.

I chided the rider for his recklessness. 'I keep forgetting,' he replied. I guess he didn't think it was important. Just because you're amid other cyclists doesn't make it any wiser to ride dangerously or discourteously.

Group recklessness causes people who should know better to cross the centre line, fail to look behind before swinging off the front of a paceline (and into the path of overtaking traffic), run red lights, ride side by side in a way that keeps motorists from overtaking them, make all sorts of bizarre and ad hoc right turns, and earn the enmity of motorists. Just the image cycling doesn't need.

Bad riding is just as lethal in groups as it is alone. A woman was killed a few years ago during a century near my home when she crossed the centreline to join other riders milling around a rest stop. She was a very experienced rider, with many credentials as a tour leader and more miles than I'll ever have, and a moment of inattention left her dead.

I generally avoid the company of reckless groups, and I don't hesitate to mention it—politely but firmly—when I see riders behaving dangerously. Most people appreciate it when someone sticks up for safe riding. Don't ever let other's company stop you being attentive.

to trust you, and you have to be smooth and predictable enough to deserve that trust. You have to lead him through a safe path. You can't wobble, swerve abruptly, or change speed without warning. Erratic movements on your part could lure him into potholes, or to touch wheels.

If you touch wheels, he'll probably go down, and you probably won't. His front wheel is pushed out from underneath him quicker than he can react. You'll feel a dull thud on your rear wheel.

You avoid touching wheels by adopting a safe following distance. Novices like to draft around three feet away; good riders usually settle on 12 to 18 inches; expert riders reduce the clearances to mere microns. Fred DeLong, the well-known cycling author and authority, tells of training rides he went on back in the 1930s; riders would have a constant *pffft pffft* noise from their front tyre just nudging the lead rider's rear tyre!

The closer you draft, the better the wind shadow you get. Theoretically, there is a good wind-break effect several bike lengths back, but cross-winds always push it off to one side. Even on days that feel dead calm, there are cross-winds—and you won't be able to find the lead rider's wind shadow more than a few feet back.

You shouldn't draft closer than is safe for your skill level and that of your companion(s), but always try to draft as close as you can. The saving in effort is one reason; another is that close formation promotes crisper, more precise riding. In the early spring after a winter of scant riding, I draft at around two feet; later in the season, when I feel sharper, I might tighten that up to a foot.

When I first started training in packs I tended to dangle around three feet off the back. This might not seem so bad, because three feet gives a reasonably good wind shadow for the following rider. But it didn't work at all. Staying that far back didn't keep me alert enough. I'd let my attention wander just a little bit, three feet all too easily became four or five, the wind shadow deteriorated, my speed dropped, and suddenly five feet became fifty. I was on my own, and I had to chase. If I did catch up, I'd be dead tired and unable to maintain the group's pace. If I didn't catch up, either my companions had to wait for me or I had to finish the ride alone—all because I let my concentration lapse.

Good riders are usually intolerant of this, because it interrupts their rhythm—and the beauty of that rhythm is something they crave. So, sticking close reminds you to pay attention. The tighter the formation, the easier you can maintain it with precision, and the less often you'll let a space develop and get dropped.

How do you stay on a wheel through thick and thin, as the lead rider goes up and down hills, over bumps, around corners, and jams across the flats? Concentration and handling skills are essential, but you have to anticipate, and the lead rider has to help you.

There are several things you as lead rider can do to make life easier for those in your slip-stream. The first is simply to stay a healthy distance away from the pavement edge. If you ride close to the edge, the following rider can't see any pavement to your left. And if he needs an escape route to the left he has to leave the pavement. (When I find myself riding with someone who hugs the pavement edge when he takes his turn at the front, I position myself to his right—slip-stream or no slip-stream. I won't ride where I can't see.) So when you're leading, place yourself far enough from the pavement edge that the following rider can see to both sides of you.

The next thing is to be as gradual as possible with all changes in course and speed. If you want to go faster, don't accelerate abruptly. Do it gradually, so that the rider following you can keep up more easily. Don't speed up when you're going to have to brake 30 yards later—that just fatigues and annoys the following rider. Take a sensible path through curves and around corners, so that the other rider can stay on your wheel.

Point to potholes and other obstructions. Some people just wiggle their finger downward, so you know an obstruction is coming up on that side. A better method is to point directly at the obstruction several times as you approach it, so the following rider can tell by your hand signal how close the obstruction is. That makes it easier for him to pay attention to the pothole and avoid it, allowing him to devote more attention to riding crisply. And it doesn't require any more effort on your part.

Both riders should verbally announce significant information. Some cyclists say 'car back' every time an overtaking car appears. If you're listening for car engines yourself, and you're already riding in a manner appropriate to being overtaken by a car, the announcement is so much unnecessary noise pollution. But if you're doing something you need to change, like riding side by side or momentarily daydreaming, the announcement is welcome.

When you're the following rider, you need to stay alert. It's critical that you sense the other rider's changes in speed and react just the right amount. If he's speeding up, you speed up just enough to stay with him. Don't pedal too hard and then jam on your brakes. Ditto if your leader is slowing down. When you overbrake and then have to chase, or accelerate too much and then have to brake, you're squandering the most valuable 'cream' of your energy. You have only so many good sprinting pedal strokes per day; don't waste them warming up your brake pads. You can usually anticipate when your leader is going to speed up or slow down. A nice, smooth downhill, the sound of a derailleur upshifting, someone's rear end getting out of the saddle and twitching happily—all portend more speed. When traffic, a busy road junction or a steepening climb looms ahead, the leader will naturally ease off.

This sounds obvious, but even experienced riders need to remind themselves of it. I found this out once when I was leading another rider up a gradual climb, approaching a stop sign. I eased off the pressure on my pedals—I hadn't yet stopped pedalling or started braking—and he ran into my rear wheel and fell. Fortunately, he suffered only a few scrapes. But even those could have been avoided if he'd watched where he was going and thought about the next logical step. Instead, he was focusing too narrowly on my rear wheel.

When I'm drafting a rider or group of riders and the pace picks up, I try to anticipate the change before they've opened up a gap, and match their speed with two strong pedal strokes. It may take three or four pedal strokes if they're really hammering, but it seldom takes more than that. The worst fate is to hesitate or daydream, discover yourself dangling off the back, and spend the next quarter of a mile sprinting at top effort, trying to get back on. Usually, two or three strong pedal strokes save me from that fate, even though I'm riding with people much faster than myself. (Note another requirement: you must always be in the right gear, or you won't be able to accelerate quickly enough.)

Your two to four pedal strokes may have to be extremely strong ones, all-out efforts,

PRACTICE MAKES...

This chapter is full of admonitions to practise little skills—braking, jumping potholes, steep U-turns. But when? Riding time is precious.

There are always spare moments. When you meet with friends for a club ride, make games out of these tasks while you wait for the departure time. Another good time is when you're nearing the end of a long hard ride and you're warming down. You're going slowly anyway, and it's an excellent time to pit your frayed muscles against co-ordination tasks.

and therein lies a rub: people who come to cycling from aerobic sports like running and swimming will have to readjust their habits. A runner never tosses in an all-out sprint in the middle of a long run. With those habits embedded, a runner-turned-cyclist can be reluctant to sprint when he needs to put in the effort to stay with another rider. But that's what you have to do. Better to stay with your companion(s) and feel completely exhausted than to keep some energy in reserve and get dropped.

The reason why is simple: such 'complete' exhaustion is temporary. With some practice, you can rest, and rest a lot, while you're on the bike. The first time I really noticed this, I was in the middle of the field in a small training race, going downhill, drafting a faster rider and coasting. Thanks to that other rider, I was passing people. I relaxed. And I could feel my heart, lungs, and muscles getting a few precious seconds to recover from the previous uphill—all while I was passing hard-working riders!

You can do the same. Get right on someone's wheel and relax, and you can often rest and recover from the effort it took to get on that wheel. There's no magic to resting. You just have to get right in where the slip-stream is best, and then squelch the tendency to be tense. If you're on a descent, you probably won't even have to pedal.

Of course, you don't need a downhill to use the slip-stream to relax and rest. You can recover when you're on the flats and must pedal yourself. You'll rest better by shifting into a slightly higher gear and pedalling slower than normal. Why? If you're drafting closely, you should require very little pedal effort to stay on the other rider's wheel. Upshift, and your pedal pressure will still be slight. And the slower leg motion saves energy, since it takes energy just to move your leg mass around.

Let's look at how a typical single-file paceline, with you and some companions of equal fitness, moves down the road. First you warm up at a moderate pace—something I'll harp on in a later chapter. When you hit full stride, the lead rider will generally be going faster than he could cruise for a long time by himself. When he's finished showing off, he swings off and attaches himself to the rear of the group, where he rests up for his next pull. The second rider, by default, gets his turn at the front, swings off, and the cycle repeats itself. This is the same whether you have two riders or 20.

But there are a thousand ways to screw it up. Every step along the way presents opportunities for the group to become unglued and unco-ordinated. The most common problem

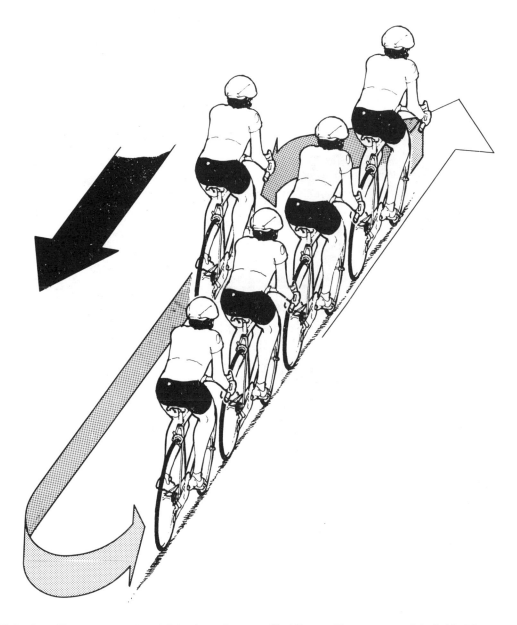

Swinging off: pull to the right fairly abruptly, ease off while paceline passes, tuck in behind last rider, and accelerate to speed with one or two pedal strokes.

is that the lead rider takes a too-long pull. Top racers take pulls of 20 or 30 pedal strokes—that's only 20 seconds—and then swing off.

Too many weekend warriors show off their stuff by hammering at the front for several minutes. In so doing, they bog down the entire group. They'll inevitably slow down after a minute—there's no escaping the destiny of human biology—and slow the whole group

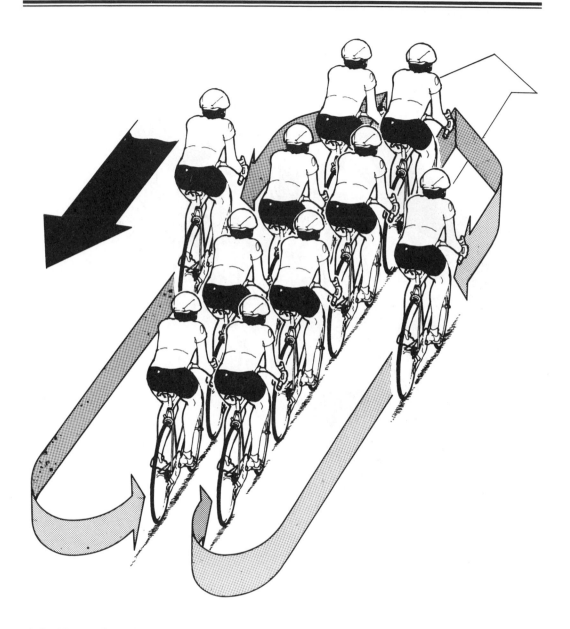

A double paceline is four riders wide when the leaders swing off; don't use it when traffic is heavy, or on narrow roads.

down with them. When they finally do swing off, they may be too tired to recover easily.

Accordingly, the best advice is to swing off frequently. Count your pedal strokes, or tell yourself you'll pull until that next crest in the road. When you're ready to swing off, look over your shoulder for overtaking traffic. (If there is traffic then stay where you are until it's clear. Safe and courteous road sharing is more important than your workout.)

Swing two feet to the right in a fairly abrupt move. It has to be abrupt, because if you

A chain gang is a constantly rotating double paceline, right side always advancing and left side always falling back (left advance, right back, in the UK). It is difficult to do but very fast.

just drift to the right, your companions may not recognize that you're swinging off. Now you're beside the paceline. Ease off your pedals and let the other riders pass by you. Tuck in behind the last rider, and accelerate to paceline speed with one good pedal stroke—two

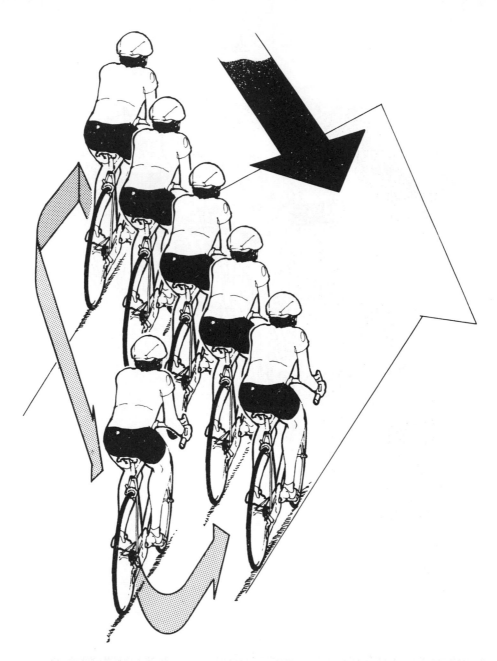

In a cross-wind riders form a diagonal echelon. Lead riders swing off across the back of the pack.

at the most.Technique is everything here; the more crisply riders tack on, the less energy they waste dangling off the back, and the faster the paceline can go.

Now relax, and follow the leader until it's your turn again. When the rider in front of you swings off, don't accelerate. Continue riding the speed the group has been riding.

If the wind is from the right (left in the UK), the leader stays close to the kerb, and still swings off across the back of the pack

Often I've seen riders drop each other by sprinting through the hole, when someone swings off. If the less refreshed riders in the rear can't sprint too, they get dropped. That's no way to treat your friends—pull through smoothly, without any change in speed. Count your pedal strokes and swing off again.

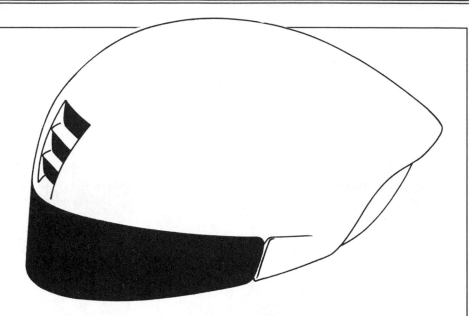

HELMETS HELP HEADS

Once I saw two riders approach each other in Central Park.

They didn't see each other, or if they did, they didn't work out what to do about it. They collided and fell. Both landed on their heads.

One rider had a helmet. I saw him again, still on his bike, hours later that day. The other rider had no helmet. We bystanders had to shoo traffic aside until the ambulance came and took her and the lump on her head away.

The moral, however boring: a helmet will usually let you finish the ride when you do land on your head.

Today's helmet choices have improved vastly over those of only a few years ago. Styles, colours, weight, and ventilation are much better.

Moreover, there used to be huge differences in protection among various helmet designs. Those differences have been greatly narrowed, thanks to the American National Standards Institute, whose Z-90.4 helmet standard has become widely accepted.

In a nutshell, this standard ensures that a helmet absorbs the energy from an impact of some severity. Specific lab tests apply a big impact to the helmet and measure the amount of that impact that would be transferred to your head. Some earlier helmet designs absorbed little impact, and I'm glad to see those designs driven from the market by the ANSI standard.

A few British firms have started to produce cycling helmets, but the majority are still imported from America. The most popular models are made from foam and fabric and weigh almost next to nothing. Can something so lightweight be strong enough to provide real protection? The answer is uneqivocally yes, so long as it has an ANSI-2-90.4 sticker.

Usually, when I hear, 'Authorities say this is safe,' I get scared. The ANSI helmet standard is a refreshing exception to this rule.

What do you do if it's your turn at the front and you're too tired? When the person ahead of you swings off, swing off with him and stay on his wheel, tacking onto the back of the group with him. If you're legitimately pooped, no one will mind. If you're just being lazy, you'll annoy the other riders.

What do you do if the person at the front just sits there and tires himself, refusing to swing off? Go around him and tack yourself onto the front. This is hard to do neatly—you have to ride faster than the group, put yourself at the front, ease off so the group gets on your wheel, and then re-establish your speed. That's one reason why the preferred method is for the front rider to swing off. At times, you'll want to ride side by side—either to chat with a friend or because your group is big enough to ride double file. A double paceline is a bit tougher for a novice than single file, but not overly so. You do need a good sense for when it is appropriate

The law on riding side by side varies from country to country , but you'll probably find that the law takes a back seat to practicality. On a lightly travelled road, with plenty of room and visibility for overtaking, do as you like. On a well travelled road where motorists can pass a single line of riders, but not a double line, you'll want to be good citizens and stay with the single line

There are other situations, however, where thought is called for. Suppose you have ten riders on a very narrow, curvy road. A motorist can't overtake even one cyclist, let alone ten, without going into the oncoming lane. The danger is that the motorist will pass where visibility is poor, overtake half of your group, and then meet oncoming traffic and dodge back to the left. If you double up, you make your train half as long, and therefore much easier to pass. You'll be doing yourself and the motorists a favour.

In a double paceline, the leading left rider customarily swings off to the left, and the leading right rider to the right. During the transition, the group is four bikes wide—enough to earn the ire of many a policeman, so use discretion.

Chain Gangs

Another type of double paceline, sometimes called a chain gang, is considerably faster, although more difficult to ride properly. It never gets more than two bikes wide. The left column of riders is always advancing and the right column of riders is always falling back. As soon as you reach the front of the right column, you swing off to the right column seconds later, another rider swings off in front of you. As soon as you reach the back of the left column, you swing into the left column and speed up; another rider will do so right after you

The beauty of a chain gang is that no one has to do the work. As soon as your turn at the front begins, it's over. That's why they go so fast. The speed of a conventional paceline is limited by the lead riders' ability to charge into the wind. The speed of a chain gang is limited only by how fast the riders can go while drafting, and by their co-ordination. Manoeuvres have to be crisp, or the chain gang falls right apart

In a cross-wind, riders stack up in a diagonal echelon (line) behind the lead rider. The wind shadow is off to one side; you ride where it will be. The rider behind you does the same. Thus, if the wind is blowing across the road from right to left, the lead rider has to be out towards the centre of the road to allow his companions to draft. If the wind is blowing from left to right, the leader should ride close to the edge; following riders will stagger themselves towards the centre line. In this instance, the leader will want to drop off the front of the group by moving sideways towards the kerb. It's far easier than swinging out around all those other riders

You can combine echelon and chain gang formats to have a constantly rotating, double echelon group of riders. You'll go much faster than you thought possible on a bike.

THE ART OF GROUP RIDING

How many people make a good group? It can be from three to 12 depending on the individual riders, their temperaments, and the roads you'll be riding.

Larger groups can go faster, but they also have disadvantages: there's a greater possibility that someone will be late or that someone will have a flat. Larger groups take up more space on the road; when you have six riders or more, you'll want to ride double-file most of the time. On narrow streets with brisk traffic, small groups may be more enjoyable and practicable.

It's fun to ride with people whose ability matches yours. That always improves the flow. But you'll also find yourself riding in heterogeneous groups, and this demands some consideration for your riding companions.

If one of your riders is barely hanging in there and needs to back off a bit, it's easier to convince a smaller group to be considerate. All too often in a large group, someone will go to the front and put the hammer down, ten others will chase, and the less fit rider will be left alone.

When the few fittest people set the pace, the less fit, less experienced riders are frustrated. They're in a losing battle, trying to learn drafting technique when they're dog tired and drowning in oxygen debt. Drafting is scary to novices, and drafting at high speed is scarier. You can't expect them to do it well when tired and worried about the speed.

On the other hand, a large group that does keep a moderate pace is the best way to teach paceline riding to a novice. The novice is forced to pay attention and stay up with the group, instead of hoping that his friends will wait for him while he fumbles with his derailleurs.

I used to join a group of ten or 12 racers who met every Thursday for a 22-mile ride. It was the day after the racers' weekly hard workout, and by agreement, the ride was at a moderate pace—probably 19 or 20 mph on the flats, slowing down appropriately on climbs. The racers got to loosen up their legs and relax, novices got to see what a paceline was like when it wasn't going 30 mph, and we got a chance to chat and enjoy ourselves. As a result, quite a few people became good riders.

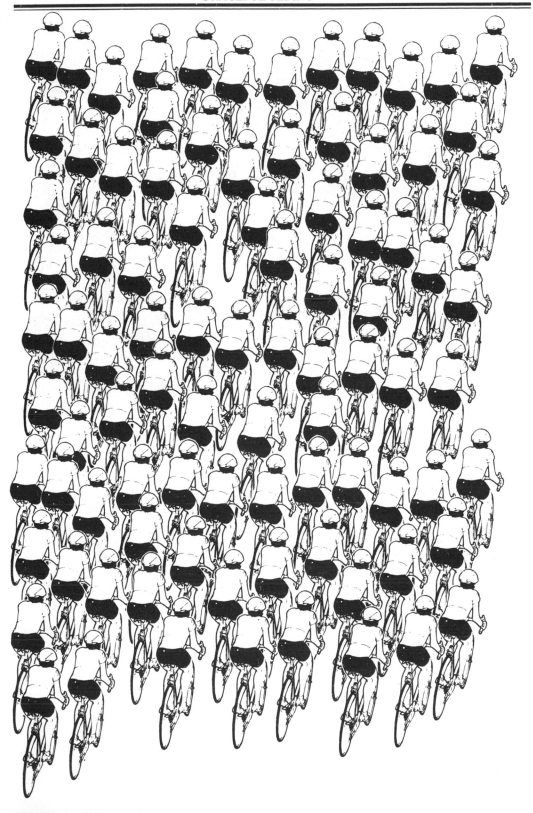

Elements of a good work-out

Contents

Assembling The Techniques

It's time to assemble the many bits of riding technique into good work-outs, and good work-out schedules. Work-outs need to fit in around your job, your social and family obligations, and your own need for sanity. The right schedules make the best of limited time to make you a bike rider.

Early Season

I've harped on the fact that you can't be a great bike rider by grinding big gears. But how can you get fit, and have the satisfaction of feeling like you've really flogged yourself (if that's what you want), by twiddling those sissy little gears?

Anything is hard work if you do it long enough. But the beauty of bike riding is that it doesn't have to feel like hard work. Ex-runners may have a tough time adjusting to cycling, because the feet and joints won't feel so flogged. Heart, lungs, and muscles, however, will have the same beneficial work-out, and joints will last longer.

Professional cyclists spend the first two months of each season twiddling little gears. They do it because it works—not just for each season, but for the rather long professional careers these riders have.

Here is a typical early season ride. For me, the distance will be anywhere from 15 to 50 miles. Novices will need to work up to 15-mile rides, but it doesn't take long. Fifteen miles is a good minimum to warm-up, get in some good pedal pounding, and warm-down. Shorter rides won't hurt, but for basic aerobic capacity and endurance, a minimum of one hour, or 15 miles, brings big dividends.

At the start of my ride I put the bike in a pretty low gear (40 to 50 inches) and start twiddling. My forward speed is slow—a good runner could pass me—but that's part of warming up. I twiddle for about two minutes, then shift up to another low gear (65 inches or so) which I can spin easily.

Why a slow start? A warm-up gets your blood pumping and your muscles warm and loose. It helps you go faster later on, because active blood circulation carries away lactic acid generated by your muscles. If you go hard from the first pedal stroke and build up lactic acid before you have blood circulation, your body will be trying to catch up for the duration of your ride. Many blood vessels in your muscles are so narrow that blood cells have to pass through one at a time, like a stack of slowly moving poker chips, and the circulation in these blood vessels may be extremely poor when you're not exercising. By warming up slowly you fill the vessels with a stack of blood cells instead of a supply of lactic acid.

The warm-up doesn't last forever. After two more minutes, I'm ready for another up shift and something closer to normal cruise speed. At this point, I'll have a cadence around 95 rpm (it varies some with terrain) and the pressure I'm putting on the pedals will be slight enough so that I can barely feel it, if at all.

This description of cadence and pedal effort is perhaps the most important objective for a new cyclist to work towards. It may be different from your idea of a good, hard work-out, but for reasons given below, it's the key to faster, better riding and fitness. I don't hit my full cruising effort until 10 or 15 minutes have passed. A long warm-up builds a good foundation for a good, lusty work-out.

But in an early season work-out, I never hit that full effort. You warm-up over the season as much as you warm-up during each individual ride. In early season work-outs, my only goals are duration on the bike and developing a nice, quick spin. Pushing on the pedals too hard won't help. In February, I'm not in shape to go fast even if I try, and trying just hurts—it turns on the lactic acid spigots. On the other hand, covering long miles at moderate speeds is pleasant, aerobically rewarding, and it prepares you nicely for faster speeds later in the season. The benefits

Blood cell queue

from these warm up rides increase greatly as the duration of the rides reaches and exceeds two hours, and these rides set you up for better performances later in the year in several valuable ways.

Here's why: the body has two basic fuels; glucose (stored as glycogen) and fat. Glucose is the primary fuel of intense aerobic activity, so the harder you ride, the more glucose you consume. Fats, on the other hand, are fuels for lower intensity aerobic activity. By burning them, you can stretch your glucose stores to let you ride farther.

One effect of working well within your aerobic capacity is to train your body to burn the 'low octane' fuel, fat. Another effect is to increase the glycogen stores in the muscles. And a third is to improve the efficiency of oxygen delivery from the blood to the muscle itself.

Training your body to burn fats is important because the body's natural tendency is to use the limited supply of glucose first, since it is more easily released. You combat this tendency with long, low-key, steady-state rides that train the metabolism to burn fat more readily. This means that you can get better performance later in the season too—without using as much glucose. The benefits increase after two hours or so because it takes about

WHAT IS LACTIC ACID?

If you exert yourself within your aerobic ability, your muscles use oxygen from the bloodstream. But if you want more horse-power than your heart and lungs can supply oxygen for, your muscles metabolically 'borrow' future oxygen. They do that by converting glucose to pyruvate and into that undesirable byproduct, lactic acid.

The lactic acid is liberated in your bloodstream and, like most acids, it hurts. That's one source of the muscle pain you feel after a burst of hard exercising. The pain goes away slowly, as your blood is pumped through the lungs, where oxygen is used to burn the lactic acid and convert some of it back to glycogen.

two hours for your glucose to be exhausted. You want to log plenty of riding miles when your glucose supply is on the reserve tank.

However, do not make early-season rides so long that they utterly deplete your glucose supply. When that happens, you get the bonk—total exhaustion. You feel just dreadful, completely drained. You don't need to bonk to train your fat metabolism. Merely approaching the bonk will suffice.

Easy early season rides also train your nervous system and synapses to the muscles. Muscles, unless trained otherwise, will use only a favoured few of their fibres. The favourite fibres contract; the other fibres act as dead weight. When those fibres aren't used, the nerves which innervate them become rusty and function poorly. Training assigns the lax fibres to active duty—a promotion they aren't capable of achieving on short notice.

To train fibres and nerves, you must first tire out the favourite fibres. Then, to keep on going, the muscles are forced to call on the other fibres and those rarely used nerves and muscle fibres get accustomed to working for a change. Again, this effect takes hold with longer work-outs, and isn't nearly so obvious in shorter rides, no matter how intense.

The little capillaries which feed these muscles are trained, too. They may be shut from disuse, but long, gentle rides will open them.

THE BIG FIXED

The undisputed king of early season workouts is fixed gear training. This is when the bike is set up with no freewheel—if the bike is moving, you're compelled to pedal. Train with a low gear around 62-65 inches on long, flat routes and you'll build up more of a spin than you thought possible, become much better at handling a bike, and have greater endurance and snap when you switch back to a geared bike.

Anybody can benefit from training on a fixed gear bike. The only hurdle is getting the equipment. Most riders use their regular bike and install a new rear wheel with a fixed-cog track hub. Some people just buy a track cog and spin it onto the freewheel threads of their existing road hub—a convenient method, since the threads are the same. But there is nothing to prevent the cog from unscrewing (the track hub has a lock ring). Either method requires you to make sure the cog is lined up directly behind the chainwheel; i.e. you can't ask the chain to work at an angle, the way it does with derailleur gearing. Aligning the chainline is likely to require special tools, shims and spacers, and ingenuity.

An alternative, which requires less fiddling with the hardware, is to set your derailleur so it's stuck on one low gear. Then you have the option of coasting, although you try to avoid it.

You don't often see ordinary cyclists riding fixed-gear. I suppose that's because you have to fuss with the equipment. But it's well worth the trouble.

Spend January and February doing your early season miles on a fixed gear, and you'll be the fastest thing around in July.

Another neurological benefit is training the co-ordination of spinning. Early season spinning trains you in that co-ordination—much like people practising their golf swing.

If you're a novice, a gentle early-season riding programme helps you get used to other aspects of the bike. Every new rider needs to firm up his bum so the saddle feels comfortable. Other parts of you—your finger muscles, your neck, your arms, and back—may benefit from some easy riding time.

Yet another benefit is psychological. Rare is the rider who can hammer all season without feeling stale. I'm sure you've known athletes who put their shoulder to the wheel hard, all year round, and don't progress much. More successful athletes avoid that.

One of the best veteran racers I know insists on moderately paced touring throughout the autumn and winter. He's in shape to ride much faster, but he likes the change of pace, and he knows that he's ultimately faster because of it. He's old enough to be my father, and when we ride together in the cold months he rides gently, but in the summer he can drop me like a stone.

Playing with cadence is a major component of early-season work-outs—seeing how fast you can pedal and feel smooth.

Why work on cadence if you're already capable of comfortable spinning at 90 rpm? To get even more comfortable. And you want to feel smooth and comfortable spinning much faster, so you can sprint to make a traffic light or pass someone in a race. Sprinting takes you up to 120 or so, and track sprinters will go still higher, to 140 or 150. The ultimate training goal is to be smooth at cadences up to 180 rpm—the bench-mark for the excellent sprinter. Much of this you'll do on rollers—the magic tool to make your cycling style creamy smooth. But much of it takes place on the road. Not much ceremony is involved; just gear down and rev up your legs.

When you do a high-cadence binge, you are in for a surprise: spinning becomes very rough and choppy at around 120 rpm, and then relatively smooth again around 135 rpm. Why? 120 rpm is at a frequency which unfortunately coincides with the resonant frequencies of your innards. Like the bridge, which was torn down by its own vibrations in moderate winds, your body organs jiggle with a vengeance when excit-

BEGINNERS: ANYTHING IS POSSIBLE

The new rider, for whom a few miles make every body part hurt, the notion of people comfortably riding dozens of miles may be nearly unbelievable.

But with practice, you improve. The body adapts.

Start with short rides that stay within your comfort zone. The range will vary widely from one individual to the next. A person who's already fit from other sports may be ready for 20-mile rides right away. Or he may need to get a tender backside used to the bike with half-mile get-acquainted rides. If you need half-mile rides, take them! (Think of a person just learning the guitar; his fingers hurt after only a few minutes of plucking the strings.)

At least three days a week, preferably more, get on the bike and take your short ride. Within a few rides, your rear end will be better acquainted with the saddle, and your leg muscles comfortable with the pedalling motion. You'll start to become familiar with the hand controls, so they don't feel foreign.

Soon enough, your rides will expand to one mile, then two, then five. You'll already be riding faster. And you'll be on to the regular training schedules in this book.

ed at the frequencies generated by pedalling at 120 rpm. Pedal faster, and you reach a frequency which no longer excites your organs. The work-out ends much as it started, with moderate effort and pace. Remember, its goal is duration and not much else.

These easygoing work-outs are an excellent excuse to have fun with your bike. Go somewhere. Have a picnic. Visit friends in the next town and get a work-out each way. Go riding with friends who aren't such tenacious cyclists—you're in no hurry, so you can enjoy their company—and let them laugh at your low gears and churning legs. Tell them that's how World Professional Hour Record Holder Francesco Moser trains, and he's the absolute king of aerobic output.

If you're a runner new to cycling, you may not feel like you've had a worthwhile work-out. After 30 miles of gentle cycling, your legs won't feel pounded. In fact, you may feel

120 rpm tummy

refreshed—after all, your heart and lungs have been pumping oxygen-rich blood through-out your body. But for proof that you've had a good work-out, put on your running shoes and head down the block. Your get up and go will be mostly gone, and you'll realize that your system is tired—a largely biochemical phenomenon. You're sure to feel mellow that evening and sleepy that night. A cycling work-out will leave you tired, but not hurting. Next time, you'll recognize that tired cyclist feeling. It's more subtle than fatigue from running.

While riding, it is hard to distinguish the deceptively subtle changes in sensation you get from changes in work-load. Suppose you're cruising at an effort level somewhat below your maximum aerobic capacity. You shift up and accelerate, maintaining the same cadence, riding at a higher speed and an effort level very slightly above your aerobic capacity. You won't feel much; perhaps a slight change in the way the muscles feel. Only after a minute or two do the big changes come home to roost: deep breaths, a pounding heart, and the realization that you've just burned up glucose anaerobically and generated a bunch of lactic acid

Teach yourself to detect that slight change early on, before the accumulation of lactic acid slows you down and disrupts your rhythm. Everybody does some rides, particularly early season rides, in which they want to stay below maximum aerobic capacity. More ambitious riders will want to go above that point at one time or another. For these riders, knowing the threshold is important, because there are times you'll want to hover just above it.

There's an even more subtle change you want to feel for: the difference between con-suming mostly fat (low intensity aerobic activity) and consuming mostly glucose (high intensity aerobic activity). (When you go anaerobic, you consume almost all glucose.) There's no clear dividing line. At best, this is an ephemeral, zen-like 'listening to your body' sensation, and I have no proof that a rider can feel it directly. But some riders I know believe they can. At the very least, they learn to recognize the difference between the effort level which leaves them limp after using up all their glycogen (which takes about two hours, depending on the individual) and the effort level which lets them keep on going after that.

Midseason

Your goals will determine how much your midseason rides differ from the deliberately easy, early season rides.

They needn't differ at all. If you want to enjoy scenery riding your bike, and shoo off heart attacks, riding will never be hard work; instead, it will be your counterpart to the cur-rent walking craze. There's mounting evidence that gentle exercise produces as much overall health benefit as far more strenuous exercise, and that holds as true for cycling as it does for walking—without the skeletal fatigue of walking. Moreover, you can go places on your bike. I know riders who complete long tours and centuries without ever working themselves hard. And their elapsed time for the centuries is often surprisingly close to that of riders who work themselves too hard and forget to relax.

Traditionally, people who don't ride very hard are assumed to have poor bike handling skills, and that's usually been the case. But if you develop those skills, your riding will be quicker and more expert at a comfortable level. And you'll be able to enjoy the company of faster riders because you'll know how to hold their wheel. Gracefulness, smoothness, and attention to detail will make you more efficient—and faster.

Harder

But what if you like the feeling of going fast, and are willing to experience a little lactic acid to tell yourself proudly, 'I just ate that hill for breakfast.' What if you crave improvement as measured by the stopwatch?

For you, a higher effort level will kick in after one or two weeks of easy twiddling. Each day's long warm-up still applies, but when you're truly warmed up, you'll want to go faster and harder. This generally means same cadence, higher gear, and flirting with that burning feeling in your legs.

Now you're entering the realm of long, steady distance, or LSD. What you want to do is steady mileage very near your aerobic threshold. You'll be right at the point where your breath is getting a little short; if you're riding with another person, you won't have the energy to converse.

Feeling correctly for this effort level is where many novices trip up. It's all too easy to fall into the trap of pounding too high a gear in quest of a little bit of hurt. After all, every other sport from rowing to tennis feels a bit gruelling when you're broadening your aerobic horizons. But if you try to simulate that feeling on a bike, you'll only be able to keep it up for a minute or two. Then the lactic acid will bring you down to reality.

Even for an expert, staying right at the anaerobic threshold is seldom easy. In addition to the fact that the cues from your own body are subtle, the world around you is in flux. Hills, traffic, and changing winds force you to anticipate and shift to keep your effort constant. The only way to get good at it is to listen to your body and practice. In time, you'll get better at recognizing those subtle cues.

Whenever you do a hard work-out, you absolutely must warm-down. Before you're so tired that you drop, ease off on your effort level; the last 15 minutes of your ride should be as easy as the first 15 minutes. A warm-down helps you recover faster for the next work-out because your blood circulation remains brisk while your muscles' production of undesirable pollutants (like lactic acid) subsides. Fresh oxygen gets a chance to whisk through and clean out the crud.

The fastest of my regular riding companions is a retired racer who warms up for ten minutes, creates a sonic boom while I desperately suck his wheel (his typical flatland cruise is about 27 mph), and then sits up and takes it easy for the last third of the ride. Because he and I warm-down so extensively, we recover quickly. I can stay with him for one of his 'death rides' (he has a way with words) and ride reasonably strongly the next day. The warm-down refreshes him so much that he can ride that hard every day for months at a time, without ever skipping a day.

Schedules

Later chapters will help you fine tune your work-outs for specific goals. If you're riding centuries, you'll need food and drink which will keep you fresh for hour after hour. If you're racing criteriums, there's work to be done on your sprint. But first, a more basic

RUBBING YOURSELF UP THE RIGHT WAY

After you've finished your ride with a nice warm-down and a relaxing soak in the tub, the best thing you can do to make yourself feel better and sleep more sound ly is a leg massage. And you can do this yourself.

Massage works wonders. Try it and see. Hammer hard on an early-season ride, add a massage to your post-ride ritual, and see how refreshed you feel the next morning.

After a long ride, there's a huge supply of metabolic slag left in the muscles. Warming down helps your bloodstream pump the slag out, but a lot remains. Massaging helps push most of the remaining slag into the bloodstream, where it can be carried away.

I repeat: try it and see. The results are far more dramatic than you'd ever guess from reading. Massage makes it possible to recover from hard rides more quickly, to tolerate greater weekly mileage than you're really in shape for, and to feel especially refreshed when you do reach for that post-ride beer.

Here's how. Lie on your back—a shag pile rug or mattress is a nice touch if you have one—with your rump near a wall and your legs extended upward, heels resting on the wall. Bend one knee towards your chest and massage that leg's calf. Always work towards the heart, kneading the muscle and shaking it occasionally for variety. Switch legs and repeat. Now do both thighs.

You can do an effective massage in five minutes, and it will hasten your recovery by a day or two. Absolutely nothing beats it.

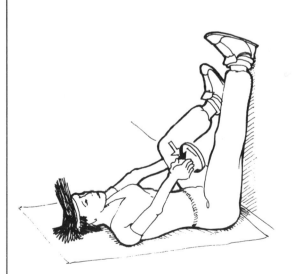

DON'T FOLLOW THE CROW

One great advantage of cycling is that you can seek out and use little-known and little-used routes, which are usually cleaner, safer, and prettier than main routes. Finding these makes the cyclist into a collector and student of maps. The best maps in the UK are published by Ordnance Survey. Use the 1:50000 scale ones in the bright mauve covers. In France, go for the little yellow Michelin maps, not quite as detailed on contour lines but the double arrows show where hills are steepest. In the USA most state tourist bureaux have cycling maps, and locally published maps and route books are often stocked in local bike shops and bookshops.

Look for maps with the correct scale and level of detail for cycling. Maps given away by oil companies are intended for motorists and leave out the best roads for cycling, those unsurfaced tracks and unofficial roads that Ordnance Survey catalogues so well

and which help to make cycling both an adventure and a pleasure.

A good source of route information is the bi-monthly magazine Cycletourist published by the Cyclists' Touring Club (Cotterell House, 69 Meadrow, Godalming, Surrey GU7 3H5). Over the years it has published hundreds of maps of members favourite rides, building up a superb library of routes. Organised on a district association basis you may find it worth joining your local DA or cycle club just to learn some new wrinkles about cycle routes in your neighbourhood. If you live in London consult the London Cycling Campaign which periodically updates its cycle route guides.

Even if you know an area well it's great fun to go through maps and pick new routes from thin little lines. Every time I unveil a new find to my friends, the response is enthusiastic. Try it—you'll make some pleasant discoveries.

problem: how do you fit riding into a tight schedule? Most people can make time for a bike ride on the weekend. But you can expect only limited success in cycling if you confine your exercise to weekends. You must do at least one weekday ride.

Half a million cyclists get their pulses pounding by riding their bikes to work. If you are one of these and take a 20-mile detour en route home once or twice per week, you have an excellent midweek training programme. But not everyone can or should commute by bicycle. All too many places of work have no shower, or no secure place to park your bike, and there are still medieval bosses who think bike riders are eccentric (a significant problem at many otherwise-decent jobs). In the UK, bicycle commuting requires a special kind of determination—something the average Chinese would never understand.

So let's assume the absolute worst thing in the world: you have to be on your way to work at 7:30, and you have weekday afternoon obligations, too.

Six a.m. never looked so good, eh?

It could be worse. First of all, it is only once a week—every Wednesday. That one work-out will balance your exercise schedule, save you from the weekend warrior syndrome, and make you a strong rider in tours, centuries, and the like. (Would-be racers will have to get up more often. To win, you must suffer.)

Second of all (morning haters take note) cycling is a good exercise for the half-awake. You do not need to be limber, and morning is the best time for riding. Fresh air and sunrises are their own rewards.

Have your bike ready, tyres pumped up, and water bottle filled, sitting by the door the night before.

Up at six, slide into your cycling togs by 6:10, groan and stretch until, at 6:15, you're on your way. At precisely 7:15 you're back. Ten minutes to shower and dress and you have five minutes to gobble breakfast.

Is it sleeting out in the morning? The routine is the same, except that you'll probably want to use an indoor training device. You can even listen to the news while you ride.

Ride gently during your early-morning ride. This is no time for heroic efforts—save that for the weekend. Go steady and easy, enjoy the scenery, and teach your body to burn fat. Do that much and you've spent the time well.

Sleep in Thursday and Friday—and spend ten minutes each day lifting weights if that's your thing. Saturday should find you rested and refreshed. That day should have the week's longest, hardest work-out. Sunday, go for a semi-long ride, but at a relaxed effort level.

A three-day per week riding schedule will bring you to the threshold of some much more ambitious riding later in the season. Here's how this might look over a period of several weeks, for a rider starting at a modest fitness level:

Week 1—total, 52 miles.
Sunday: 20 miles, easy early-season pace.
Wednesday: 12 miles, easy early-season pace
Saturday: 20 miles, easy early-season pace.

Week 2—total, 57 miles
Sunday, 20 miles, easy.

Wednesday, 12 miles, easy.
Saturday, 25 miles, easy, with a slight surge in the middle five miles and then a long warm-down.

Week 3—total, 63 miles
Sunday, 20 miles, easy.
Wednesday, 13 miles, easy, but you're getting naturally faster.
Saturday, 30 miles, easy, with five-mile surge and long warm-down.

Week 4—total, 74 miles
Sunday, 25 miles, easy.
Wednesday, 14 miles, getting a bit faster still.
Saturday, 35 miles, with a good surge and warm-down.

You can extrapolate the schedule from there. It's not particularly dramatic—you won't get to the Tour de France this way—but look what you get out of it. Your riding time is about five hours per week—a modest commitment you can live with. And yet you could have a lot of fun with the fitness you'd glean from these work-outs. You could comfortably finish a ride as long as a metric century (100 km, or 62 miles), or go pub touring 30-35 miles per day and feel fresh every day. Or you could ride to visit friends 40 miles away, stay with them, and make a return trip the next day.

In fact, I recommend that you try to dangle one of these little prizes in front of yourself. You deserve a reward, a small achievement, after a month of regular working out.

I'll return to work-out schedules later and tailor more demanding schedules to the loftier ambitions you may have. But in the meantime, let us back up a bit and look at some background information on the human engine and how it interacts with the bicycle.

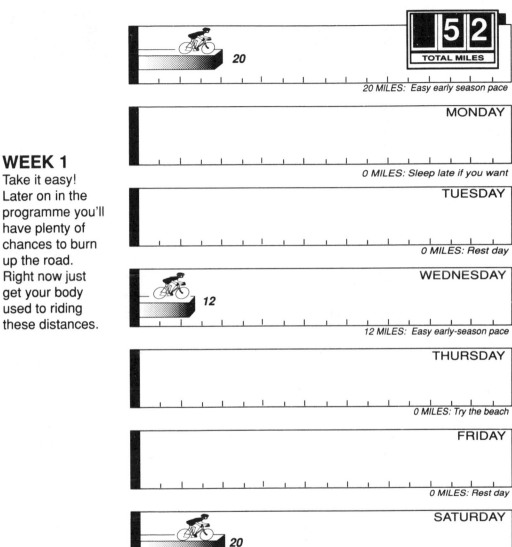

52 **TOTAL MILES**

20

20 MILES: Easy early season pace

MONDAY

0 MILES: Sleep late if you want

TUESDAY

0 MILES: Rest day

WEEK 1

Take it easy!
Later on in the
programme you'll
have plenty of
chances to burn
up the road.
Right now just
get your body
used to riding
these distances.

WEDNESDAY

12

12 MILES: Easy early-season pace

THURSDAY

0 MILES: Try the beach

FRIDAY

0 MILES: Rest day

SATURDAY

20

20 MILES: Easy early season pace

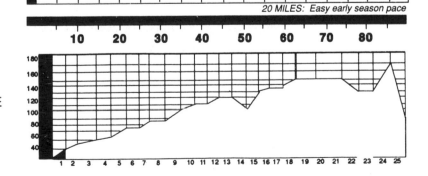

TOTAL
FITNESS BASE
MILES
52

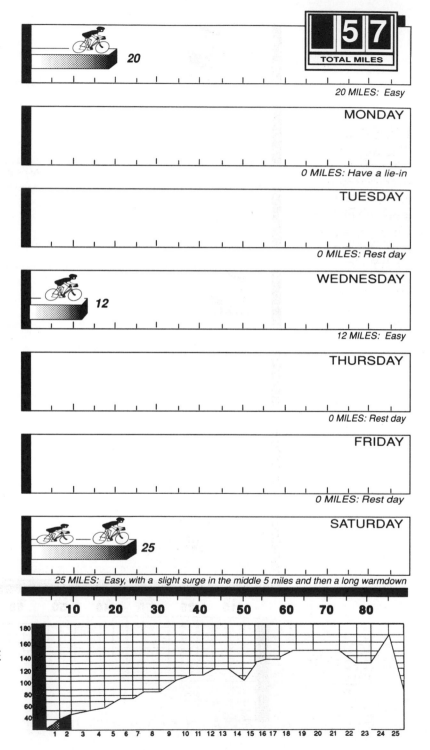

WEEK2
Saturday has
your first surge,
but keep it
modest and
do the
warm-down
completely.

5 7
TOTAL MILES

20

20 MILES: Easy

MONDAY

0 MILES: Have a lie-in

TUESDAY

0 MILES: Rest day

WEDNESDAY

12

12 MILES: Easy

THURSDAY

0 MILES: Rest day

FRIDAY

0 MILES: Rest day

SATURDAY

25

25 MILES: Easy, with a slight surge in the middle 5 miles and then a long warmdown

TOTAL
FITNESS BASE
MILES
109

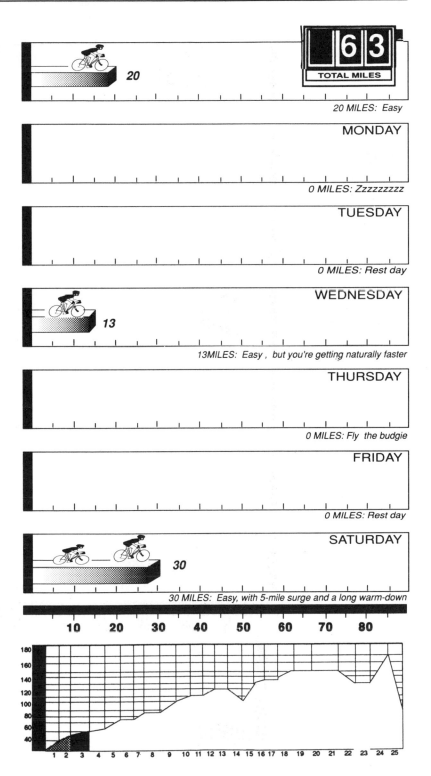

6 3
TOTAL MILES

20

20 MILES: Easy

WEEK 3

This week the miles start rolling by more easily. Give it a decent effort when you surge, but keep some strength in reserve.

MONDAY

0 MILES: Zzzzzzzzz

TUESDAY

0 MILES: Rest day

WEDNESDAY

13

13MILES: Easy , but you're getting naturally faster

THURSDAY

0 MILES: Fly the budgie

FRIDAY

0 MILES: Rest day

SATURDAY

30

30 MILES: Easy, with 5-mile surge and a long warm-down

10   20   30   40   50   60   70   80

TOTAL
FITNESS BASE
MILES
172

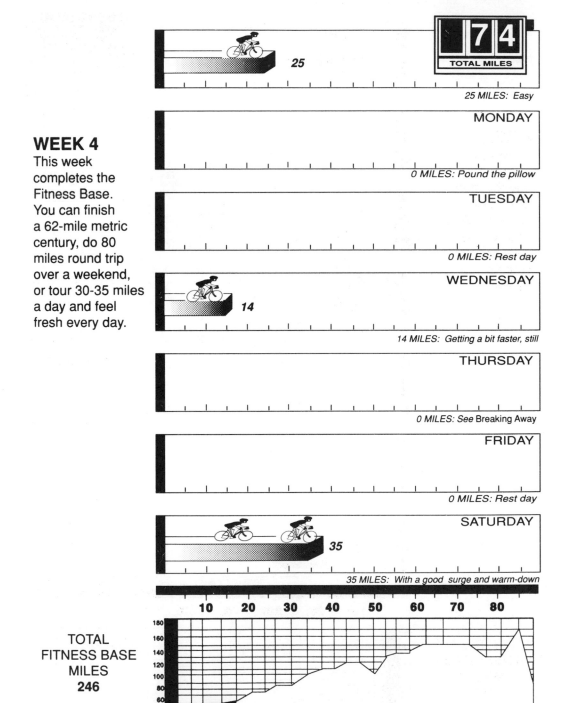

74 TOTAL MILES

25

25 MILES: Easy

WEEK 4

This week completes the Fitness Base. You can finish a 62-mile metric century, do 80 miles round trip over a weekend, or tour 30-35 miles a day and feel fresh every day.

MONDAY

0 MILES: Pound the pillow

TUESDAY

0 MILES: Rest day

WEDNESDAY

14

14 MILES: Getting a bit faster, still

THURSDAY

0 MILES: See Breaking Away

FRIDAY

0 MILES: Rest day

SATURDAY

35

35 MILES: With a good surge and warm-down

TOTAL FITNESS BASE MILES **246**

Rider Position

Contents

Adjusting Your Bike

Proper position is little short of a miracle.

Let's face it, a bicycle isn't exactly a recliner chair. The customary riding position doesn't seem to lend itself to relaxing. But, surprisingly, you can relax on a bike, and feel far better during and after your ride. Proper position is essential to make this happen.

People often make either too much or too little of position. Many custom-proportioned bicycle frames, built at enormous expense, turn out to be virtually identical to common-stock frames—a few millimetres difference doesn't really matter in most cases. Of course, some cyclists have atypical body proportions and need custom frames, and many people simply enjoy the pride of owning a custom-built bike, necessary for size reasons or not. At the other extreme, many cyclists, including avid regulars on long club rides, are on bikes so ill-adjusted that they cause their owners unnecessary pain and slow them down.

I'm going to go through the basics, explain the reasons, and give the traditional guidelines. You want seat, pedals, and handlebars in the right places, cranks the right length, shoe cleats aligned correctly, and your pronation foot roll within reasonable limits. Square these items away according to the usual rules of thumb and you'll probably have no position problems.

If your needs are more demanding than most people's, and the guidelines given here don't render you pain-free, there are several places you can turn to for further in-depth specialised work. The most common of these would be a pro bike shop, cycling coach, or custom framebuilder who has expertise in observing you on the bike and noticing nuances that could cause problems.

A few specialists have invested in a fitting programme called the Fit Kit. In the hands of a good operator, the Fit Kit is a precise tool for setting up a rider according to the usual guidelines, and it's particularly helpful for cleat placement discussed below.

If this chapter doesn't solve your position problems, your first step may be to go to a pro-shop for expert help. Before you take that step, you might as well see how close you can get on your own. You need your bike, tools to adjust the saddle and handlebars, and a friend to hold the bike upright. A wind load simulator is another handy way to hold the bike upright.

Saddle Height

The quest for perfect position starts with saddle height. Surprisingly, with the bicycle as old as it is, saddle height is still a subject for debate. Exercise physiologists continue to study power output at various saddle heights. Five-time Tour de France winner Bernard Hinault tried saddle height experiments in a wind tunnel to determine his most aerodynamic and efficient position. One surprising result: for better *aerodynamics*, he raised his saddle! It made his upper body flatter and sleeker. This increased his power output, too.

Among good racers, there's been a massive raising of saddles in this decade.

Greg LeMond, the first American to win the Tour de France in 1986, told me he raised his saddle about two centimetres higher than the old guidelines called for and many other riders have followed suit. Even so, you should start with the traditional saddle height. Learning smooth form and a brisk cadence is somewhat easier with the saddle a bit low. Also, bike handling is noticeably easier with a low centre of gravity. After you have those

With your heel on the pedal your leg should extend fully at the bottom of the stroke, without rocking the hips. With the ball of your foot on the pedal, your leg should remain slightly bent at the bottom of the pedal stroke.

skills wired, you may want to experiment, raising your saddle half a centimetre at a time.

The traditional saddle height is at a position where your knee is not quite fully extended at the bottom of the pedal stroke. To find that position, get on the bike, put your heels on the pedals, and turn the cranks. You'll have to turn them backwards if a person, and not a stand, is holding the bike upright. If you have to rock your hips from side to side to reach the bottom portion of the pedal stroke, your saddle is too high. Lower it just to the point where you don't have to rock.

When your foot is in its customary position, with the ball centred over the pedal spindle, your knee is visibly bent at all times.

People new to cycling find this position takes getting used to. It feels too low at first. A higher saddle position feels more natural, because it's more like walking.

If you're new to cycling and just learning to spin, give this 'too low' position a chance. It's natural to want your knee to lock straight with every pedal stroke, as if you were walking, but it's not good for cycling. Try the traditional setting for several rides. If you're sure you want a higher saddle position and your spin doesn't suffer, raise the saddle half a centimetre at a time. Even if it then makes you ride like Greg LeMond, you won't regret having learned to spin at the lower seat height first.

According to a 1974 study by M. Desipres 'An electromyographic study of competitive road cycling conditions simulated on a treadmill,' (*Biomechanics* IV, Nelson and Morehouse, editors, University Park Press), a higher position helps experienced riders go faster, because the leg muscles turn on earlier in the pedalling cycle, and they stay on longer. The result is more power.

However, there's a trade-off between increasing power by raising the saddle, and the overall efficiency of keeping your saddle lower. Only by getting to know yourself on the bike can you select the trade-off position ideal for you. Beware of pat answers to positioning questions; no one formula will work for every rider. Personal preferences play a part, too, and these change over time. This year, I put up my saddle about a centimetre after years of the same position. The best coaches will always set your bike up and then tell you: 'This is a starting point. Listen to your body, and if it tells you to try modifications, try them in small increments.'

Saddle Tilt

Start out with the saddle parallel to the ground. You'll probably leave it that way. Some cyclists like the nose of the saddle pointing very slightly upward—this helps you put more of your weight on the saddle, and less on your hands. Many cyclists can't stand this upward tilt—it puts pressure on your body in all the wrong places.

If the nose is tilted down, that's a sign of trouble. Some people have their saddles too high, and then tilt them down to relieve pressure on the crotch. Then they're forever bracing themselves with their arms to keep from sliding into the bars.

Saddle Fore/Aft

First set the saddle in the correct fore/aft position over the pedals, then adjust for handlebar position by changing stem length. When your pedal is in the 3 o'clock straight forward position, your knee should be directly over the pedal. Adjusting the saddle fore and aft moves your knee fore and aft. When seated on the bike, have a friend dangle a plumb bob from the front of your leg, just below your kneecap. The plumb bob should line up with the pedal spindle. This is the optimum position for exerting muscle power on the pedals.

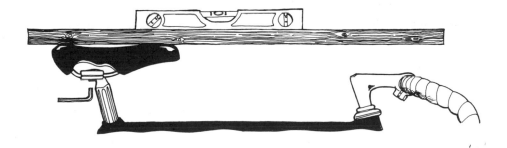

Start with saddle dead level

Knee over pedal spindle with crank at 3 o'clock position gives correct saddle fore/aft position.

Handlebar Position

Set your handlebar height for your riding style. Generally speaking, touring cyclists extend their handlebar stems up higher than racing cyclists. Then, when down on the hooks curved handlebar ends, their backs aren't bent over as far. This is an important consideration for people with stiff backs. If you crave more handlebar height than your bike's stem gives you, you can buy special stems from Nitto or SR that have an extra few centimetres of column height

Racers like their stems set down in the frame, so when they get on the hooks, they're lower and more aerodynamic. Besides, the bike looks cool when the bars are inches lower than the saddle. Watch, though, that you don't have your bars down so low that the drop position is uncomfortable to use.

The rule of thumb for handlebar fore/aft position again calls for the plumb bob. With your hands down on the hooks, hold your head up and look at the horizon. A plumb line dropped from your nose should land on the centre of the handlebars.

Make changes in fore/aft handlebar position by altering stem length. Stems range from four to 14 centimetres, but bike handling stays better if you keep within 6-12 centimetres.

You needn't be a slave to the rule of thumb. In practice, I've been comfortable on bikes which are both too long and too short to conform to this rule. Over the years, my preferred reach has shrunk about two inches, and I keep meaning to buy a shorter stem for one of my bikes. However, the rule of thumb, combined with common sense and keeping a look-out for position-related aches and pains, will show you if you're far from the norm.

Where you put your handlebars is only half the question. The other half is where you place your hands on them. The biggest single rule is: keep your arms bent. If there is no bend in your elbow, you can't be loose on the bike. Would you go skiing with your knees locked straight? If you need to lock your elbows straight to be comfortable with your hands on the hooks, the handlebars are too low and/or too far away.

You are not compelled to ride on the hooks. The fact is, most riders spend most of their time riding with their hands up higher. I favour riding with my hands on the brake hoods. It gives nice elbow bend and a moderately aerodynamic, semi bent-over position, and is comfortable for hours at a time.

The brake hood position can be used almost as you would the tops of the bars, when you want an upright and relaxing posture. Yet your hands are farther apart, for better steering control, and you can actuate the brake levers.

Practise braking from this position, and you'll be comfortable doing 90 per cent of your braking this way. Should you need to move your hands down to the hooks for emergency braking or steering, your hands are closer to that position already, so you can get there faster.

I only keep my hands down on the hooks constantly when riding time trials. At 25 mph, you can feel the increased wind resistance from any deviation from perfect aerodynamic position—so you're forced to stay shrivelled down, trying to hide behind your handlebar stem. At the end of an hour-long time trial, I'm really sick of that position!

Foot Position and Cleat Placement

The most important positioning is foot placement on the pedal. Getting it wrong can cause permanent injuries, and possibly end your cycling career. The stakes are higher than for any of the other adjustments I've mentioned above. You spend many hours with your feet locked in position, and a small error can cause big problems.

That said, it's not that difficult to get it right. Read the following carefully and take the time to ensure you're correct.

There are three aspects to foot position: fore/aft translation, rotation around a vertical axis yaw, and rotation around the straight-ahead horizontal axis roll

Fore/aft translation is the easy one: the ball of your foot should be directly over the pedal spindle.

Why? Your leg has three separate lever arms and pivot points: the thigh, pivoted at the hip; the calf, pivoted at the knee, and the foot, pivoted at the ankle. You can get considerable power out of this third pivot—your strong calf muscle's job is to point your toes downward during the pedal stroke.

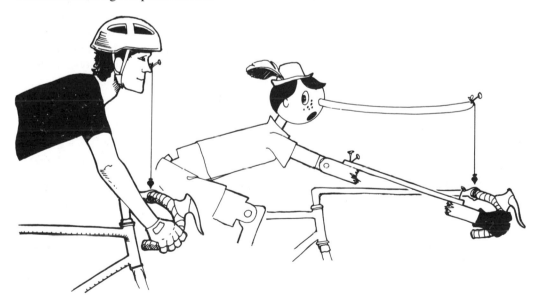

Bars too far forward stretch out the rider and can create severe back pain.

Called ankling, this will probably come naturally to you. The ball of your foot is the best place for this third lever arm to meet the pedal.

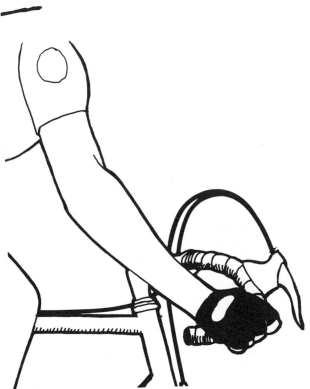

A bent arm is essential for absorbing road shock

If your foot is too far forward, you aren't using the full length of the lever arm. This is the most common problem; you often see novice riders without toe clips pedalling with their arches.

If your foot is too far backward, your toes become part of the lever arm, and they aren't suited for the job. This feels extremely uncomfortable and you'll probably notice it right away.

If you do not use cleats, toe clip size determines your fore/aft position. Your feet will naturally slide all the way into the toe clips. Clips come in small, medium, and large, with no standardization of sizes among manufacturers. Also, not all feet are proportioned equally. Your size 9 foot may have

ARE YOUR LEGS THE SAME?

Hardly anyone among us is symmetrical, and yet most of us go through life without ever learning which leg is longer than the other, or by how much. Leg length differences of less than a quarter of an inch seldom require a cyclist to make any changes to the hardware. But at some point, you want the bike to adapt to you.

You have three convenient tools to make this adaptation. The first is crank length.

It's not convenient or cheap to order an odd crank of a different length. But it does the job. If the difference in your leg length is in your thighs, then compensate for this by choosing the appropriate crank lengths.

For a difference in the lower legs, the compensation should be in the pedal cage height. One way to do this is to buy Shimano drop-centre pedals, which can be fitted only to Shimano's older aerodynamic Dura Ace crankset. The longer leg gets a drop centre pedal; the shorter leg gets a conventional pedal screwed into an adapter which fits the crankset

Another solution: France's T.A. offers orthopaedic pedals with a variety of cage heights. A good bike shop can order them for you.

its ball a centimetre farther forward than your neighbour's size 9. Find a brand and size of toe clip that fits and remember what it is. Toe clips require replacing every couple of years, and you want to buy the correct replacement size.

If you use cleats, their placement on the shoe sole determines the position of your foot. But make sure your toe clips are long enough to reach around the front of your shoes. Whether you have a space between the clip and the front of your shoes, or a snug fit, is a matter of personal preference. Some guidebooks insist on a quarter inch of space; personally I prefer a snug fit.

People with size 12 feet and beyond will probably need to use washers or blocks of lightweight plastic as spacers to extend their toe clips far enough forward.

Rotation around the vertical axis is a fancy name for whether you're pigeon-toed, toed straight ahead, or have your ankles scraping the crankarms.

You'd think you'd want your toes pointing straight ahead. Surprisingly, though, that's not the neutral position for about three quarters of the population. According to shoe designer Dave Greenbaum, neutral position for most people is off to one side or the other by a considerable distance. Ten degrees or so is typical.

Finding the neutral position for the foot is the most critical adjustment. If set out of line, your foot wobbles with each pedal stroke. That wobble is translated through your ankle to your knee, and causes the bones to grind against the inside of the kneecap. Painful injury follows. Riders without cleats will probably find that their feet naturally seek their own neutral position. Simply letting your feet do that will be enough. You may even find that your foot wants to rotate slightly with each pedal stroke. If you use touring shoes with quasi cleat-like slots, watch it! Those slots can't be adjusted, so they may force your foot to assume a position incorrect for you.

Riders with cleats have to determine the correct position in order to set the cleats. The most elegant way of doing so is with the Fit Kit's best tool, the Rotational Adjustment Device (RAD) The bike is set up on a wind trainer and the pedals replaced with the RADs.

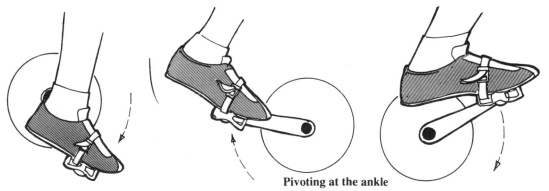

Pivoting at the ankle

These accept your feet like normal pedals, but have an extra vertical pivot which rotates freely. You pedal for a minute or so without looking at your feet, which naturally assume the neutral position correct for them. The position is indicated by a pointer on the RAD, and you then set up your cleats according to that measurement.

The conventional homebrew alternative is to ride without cleats until the pedals mark

Hip, knee and ankle pivot points

the shoe soles. The cleats are mounted so that the slots are aligned with the marks left by the rear pedal cages. If you use a wind trainer, you can speed up the process by having a friend take a pencil and trace the pedal cage lines on your shoe soles.

Cleats can loosen. Check them from time to time and make sure they haven't moved. Cycling shoes used to come without cleats, which were purchased separately and fastened on with nails. You had to be very careful when doing the mounting, because you had only one chance to get it right.

Pre-mounted, easily adjustable cleats are a great convenience, but have spawned an upsurge in cleat-related knee problems. Apparently, many people do not give any thought to cleat position and leave them where placed by the shoe factory. All too often the result is damaged knees.

One way to position adjustable cleats is to loosen them up just a little bit, so that when you have your feet in the pedals, a moderate amount of force can change the setting. This allows you to experiment with different positions; when you're comfortable, tighten the cleats firmly into place. If your neutral foot position is heavily heels-inward, you may have problems with your ankles scraping the crankarms. One solution is cutaway crankarms offering as much as an extra quarter inch of clearance. Virtually every manufacturer's current production has some cutaway models; you shouldn't have any trouble finding one.

Another solution is extra-wide pedals, which position your feet farther outboard to gain clearance. The thought may horrify; most wide pedals are cheapies made for department store bikes. However, there are a few wide well-made, sturdy aluminium quill pedals from manufacturers such as Sakae Ringyo. Be patient with your bike shop; not all models in the catalogue are actually available from wholesalers.

There is no means of adjustment on your shoes or pedals for rotation around the straight-ahead horizontal axis valgus/varus, but it's a very important position to consider and correct. This aspect of positioning has major performance-enhancing and injury-preventing possibilities.

Most people can ride comfortably with their feet in the neutral, flat position their pedals normally give. But you may not be most people.

The injuries caused by incorrect varus/valgus adjustment are cousins of injuries caused by incorrect toe in/toe out cleat adjustment. The foot, kept away from its preferred, neutral position, rotates with each pedal stroke. That motion is translated to the knee-cap as both rotation and side-to-side motion, and can cause injury. This is the same motion runners know as over-pronation.

Moreover, whenever the forces of pedalling aren't neatly perpendicular, your pedalling efficiency suffers. If your feet need to rotate outward before they start applying pressure to the pedals, that's a wasted sideways motion an energy-absorbing diversion from the task of turning the cranks.

Knee motion serves as a pointer which amplifies and shows off this wasted motion. I can see this in my own knees; they usually wag from side to side a bit at the top of each pedal stroke.

Traditional orthotics, prescribed by a knowledgeable podiatrist, can help. These are inserts for shoes that tilt the foot. However, getting them into your shoes may be easier said than done. Cycling shoes are supported at the ball of the foot, and so you need a full-length orthotic which reaches up into the toe. Most cycling shoes are too snug for a full-length orthotic to fit. One notable exception: the Cyclebinding shoe is made for orthotics users. Another approach is to put wedges between the shoe and the pedal, but that disrupts the cleat-to-pedal relationship. Yet another approach is a custom shoe—expensive and hard to find.

There's another solution. A recent and unique product from California podiatrist Harry Hlavack and cycling expert/designer Erik Koski is the Biopedal, a bicycle pedal which adjusts in varus/valgus and toe in/toe out, and in height, so you can also use it to adjust for leg length differences. If you need to experiment with these adjustments, or think you do, the Biopedal is the only product of its kind that allows you to do so.

I was fortunate enough to be examined by inventor Hlavack and the results were illuminating. He said I had generally good biomechanics and well-adjusted cleats when I arrived, but he also noticed my knee motion and documented it on videotape.

During a RAD-style adjustment session on a wind load simulator, I found my neutral position had two degrees of varus tilt lifting the inside of the foot the equivalent of giving myself an orthotic or arch support. He adjusted the Biopedal accordingly. The videos showed less wasted motion as a result.

Hlavack speculates I might save two per cent of my energy by using his pedals and remember, my biomechanics were good to start with. In his own studies, riders who use the pedal to make needed adjustments generally find themselves riding 'one gear higher'.

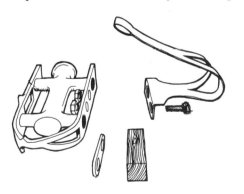

Small pieces of wood are easily trimmed to size as spacers

If he's right, many riders who currently have poor biomechanics could make quantum improvements by fixing this position. Even if he's off by a factor of four, half a per cent is a big difference. Cyclists often seek improvements much smaller than that through aerodynamic components and ultra-stiff frames.

Is the Biopedal for you? It is if you have the appropriate medical problems or the desire go to that little bit faster. It and the imitators it's sure to spawn will do wonders to alleviate cyclists' pain and speed them up.

The Terry Bicycle

SHORT WOMEN AND BIKE FIT

The riders most likely to have a problem with reach to the handlebars are short women. Women have proportionally shorter arms and torsos than men anyway, and a bike that a 5'2" man can ride may be a torture rack for a 5'2" woman. Often I've put women on bikes which had the appropriate seat tube length, but found they simply couldn't reach the bars hence, they couldn't ride the bikes.

Open frame bikes don't solve this problem. Top tube or no, there is still a long distance from seat to handlebars.

If you are overstretched on a bike, you probably know it: cycling hurts your back, shoulders and arms with constant stress. When the angle between your torso and your upper arm exceeds 90 degrees, you're reaching out for the handlebars, and you have to keep arm muscles flexed to hold your body up. You need the bars close enough to keep that angle under 90 degrees; then your bones, and not your muscles, do the work of holding you up.

American framebuilder Bill Boston invented a bicycle design for riders who have this problem; he mated a 24-inch front wheel with a 27-inch rear wheel. The smaller front wheel allows him to use a top tube about two inches smaller than you'll find on bikes with 27-inch front wheels. This design is now widely copied by mass manufacturers and is still available from Boston himself. I mention it specifically because it is the only way for many riders to get a bike that fits and you need a bike that fits.

DOING IT LYING DOWN

Would you like to ride a bike that's faster and far more relaxing than any racing bike, and yet more comfortable than some small cars? Recumbents fit that description. You sit in a supine position, not unlike a chaise longue with your feet propped upon the ottoman.

The comfort factor is impossible to argue with, as is the 65 mph speed record set by Gardner Martin's Easy Racer Gold Rush. Even without an aerodynamic body shell, the recumbent is lower and faster than a conventional bike.

Recumbents are rarities. The biggest reason why is that they look ungainly and take up more space than conventional bikes.

Recumbents suit people who can't ride upright bikes. A recumbent rider I know gets back pain on an upright bike; another has the use of only one arm and doesn't like breaking with lopsided pressure on the steering.

But there are other people who simply prefer the bikes because they're faster and more comfortable. If fitting yourself to a conventional bike is difficult, or if you want to go faster in greater comfort, a recumbent is a good way to start.

Richard's Windcheetah SL

RECORD YOUR POSITION

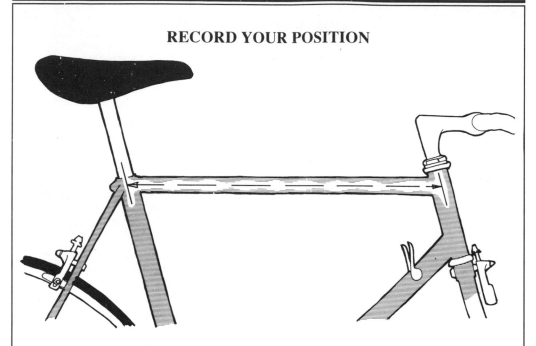

Once you've set your bike up so that it fits, take a tape measure to it and record the results. Sooner or later, you'll be glad you did.

Connie Carpenter Phinney, the 1984 Olympic Gold Medalist, was once travelling to a race when her bike was pretzeled in shipping. She hurriedly borrowed a bike for the race but didn't know the measurements for her riding position, and did not adjust the bike properly. As a result she did poorly, and hurt herself.

You may have to disassemble your bike

for shipping, or borrow a friend's bike. If you've taken the trouble to establish your correct position, you'll want to be able to re-create it easily.

The most important measurement is seat height. Whenever you remove the seat post, put a piece of tape around it to mark where it meets the frame. The other way, which is transferable to other bikes, is to measure from the crank spindle centre to the top of the saddle. (Note the crank length, too; if the new bike's cranks are five mm longer, you'll want to lower the saddle five mm.

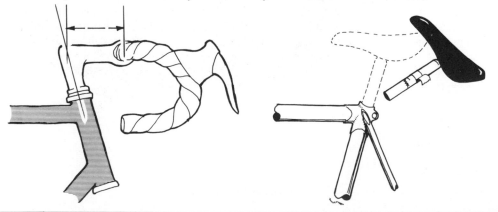

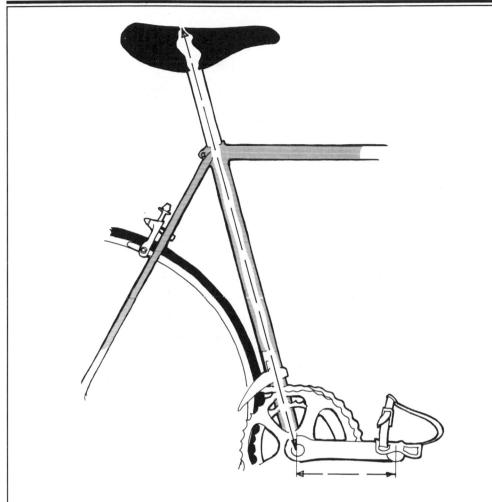

Vice versa for shorter cranks.)

Measure the top tube from the centre of the seat tube to the centre of the head tube. Measure the handlebar stem from the head tube centre to the handlebar centre. You can't change these dimensions as easily, but at least you'll know what you're used to.

Make a mental note of how handlebar height compares with seat height. This depends on frame size and on how far the handlebar stem is inserted into the head tube. Again, a change in frame size might make it difficult to duplicate your old measurement, but at least you'll know what you're working with.

● If you are an exception to the position-

ing rules in this chapter don't let fashion dissuade you from fulfilling your own needs. It's just not that important to have your bike look like everyone else's. If there's a problem, study it until you understand it, get competent medical help, and do what it takes to make yourself comfortable on the bike.

Framebuilder Peter Weigle has a knee he has to watch, and a special set-up of his own. He has a toe clip on one side and no clip on the other. He can't wear cleated shoes anymore. But he can outride many a normal rider outfitted with cleats.

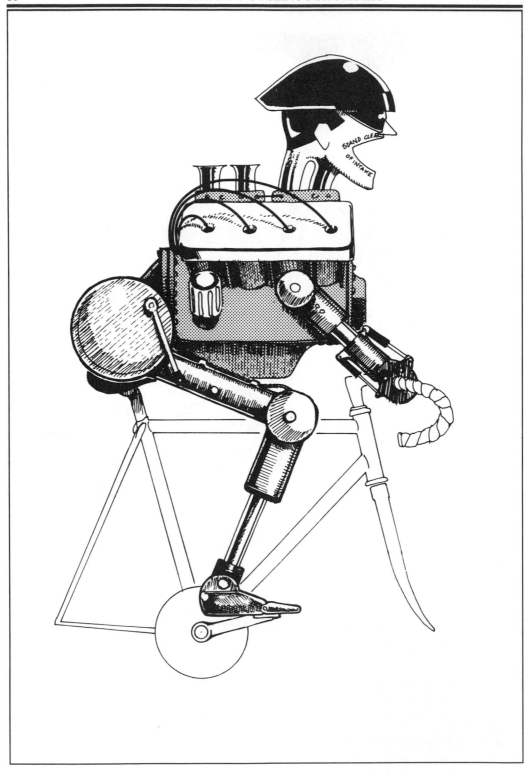

The Human Engine

Contents

High tech application of slant board

How the Body Works

Bike riding is fun for its own sake; the physiological benefits are secondary—a nice added bonus. Studying the biochemistry involved is definitely tertiary. Nonetheless, an understanding of how the body responds to exercise can help you avoid injuries and make the most of your training.

Suppose a completely sedentary person takes up a cycling programme and really sticks with it. At the beginning, he can only ride, say, 13 mph on level ground without getting winded, and that only for short distances. At the end of two years, he has worked up to 150 miles per week as a regular training schedule, dabbled in club racing, and peaked for the year at an hour-long time trial, where he maintained 23 mph. He can comfortably complete a flat 100-mile century in six hours. Nice rewards, and quite realistic for a person who's ambitious, trains regularly, and has the benefit of skilled riding companions to keep him sharp.

These external results of training are accompanied by significant changes *inside* the body. The resting pulse of our hypothetical subject—call him Mick—will probably drop from the national average of 72 to 50 or below—an indication of how much larger, healthier, and more powerful his heart has become. Also, his pulse at a given work-load will drop. However, pulse does not strictly correlate with fitness or ability to do anything else so it's possible to get in excellent shape and find your pulse never gets slow enough to brag about. Conversely, many weekend athletes in mediocre condition have resting pulses just as slow as those of world-class athletes.

Mick can burn fat instead of glucose for much of his riding, and this makes it much harder to exhaust him. The 100-mile century proves that. He has increased the fat stored in his muscles and the number of enzymes that burn it. He can also store nearly three times as much glucose in his muscles as before. His liver, however, did not increase its glycogen storage capacity. And that's the main supply.

Mick produces less lactic acid at a given work-load, because his anaerobic threshold has increased. He has more blood volume and more functional capillaries in his muscles. His blood pressure and blood cholesterol and triglyceride levels tend to decrease. 'Tend to' because riding a bike does not take the place of a healthy diet!

His lungs have increased in volume, capacity, and efficiency, but this change isn't particularly important because the lungs have excess capacity already. A one-lunged swimmer won a gold medal in the 1972 Munich Olympics.

Mick's body fat and overall weight have probably decreased slightly; his lean body mass is either unchanged or marginally increased. His bones, ligaments, and tendons are stronger in response to the stress of exercise.

The change in Mick's power output is little short of miraculous. At 13 mph Mick could deliver a modest 0.08 horsepower to the pedals. After two years he more than quadrupled that, putting out 0.33 horsepower at 23 mph.

But the unbelievable part is that exercise physiologists have proved that increases in power output are only distantly correlated with improved aerobic capacity. Aerobic training increases the ability to consume oxygen by a maximum of 20 per cent. And that's for elite athletes. The rest of us can increase our oxygen consuming ability about 13 or 14 per cent yet, like Mick, we can use that training to quadruple the energy we deliver to the pedals. Moreover, Mick's aerobic capacity did almost all of its increasing during his first weeks of training, when he went from zero to 50 miles per week. At that point, his maximum cruising speed and power output were only slightly improved. As he continued to train, his aerobic capacity did not change, but his output improved dramatically!

Well . . . what are the other factors that allow you a four-fold increase in performance?

One answer is technique; a trained cyclist's muscles apply power more efficiently. Untrained subjects waste a lot of energy fighting themselves. Some of this is visible as energy expended making the bike go everywhere but forward—continuing to push on the pedal for that tenth of a second after it's reached the bottom of the stroke, for example.

Moreover, there are some surprisingly important nuances of co-ordination which untrained cyclists need to learn. They literally push down on both pedals at once. Or they try to extend the lower leg and flex it at the same time. Sounds silly, but you probably do it, too. Midway through the pedal stroke, the leg has to switch from flexion to extension, and it gets about 1/100th of a second in which to do it correctly. It's difficult for any but the best trained athletes to do without crossing up the nerve signals and energising both opposing muscles at once. This was discovered by electromyographic tests conducted by Shimano's Shinpei Okajima during the development of the Biopace chainwheels.

If you were tested at a given work-load before and after conditioning, you'd see either no change or a slight decrease in oxygen consumption and cardiac output, due to increased mechanical efficiency and greater extraction of oxygen from the blood. That's a factor in your increased output. Another factor: you've brought more muscle cells into the act, making them full participants. This last item may be a key one. 'Change in muscles with exercise programme' is now a hot topic among researchers.

Also, as you train, your anaerobic threshold improves dramatically, even as your aerobic capacity doesn't.

You are indeed born with a ceiling to your aerobic capacity determined largely by heart stroke volume and training can't overcome heredity. The tests have shown that top racers are born with more capacity, in addition to more ability to improve that capacity, than average humans. That's why they are, literally, big-hearted. However, the fastest riders aren't necessarily the ones who do the best in lab tests. Many riders who've been very successful on the bike have performed far less well in the tests.

Aerobic capacity cannot be improved more than 15 or 20 per cent because there's a bottleneck in the oxygen-consuming pipeline: the muscle cells' ability to use oxygen. Sure, when an untrained individual begins exercise, he'll need to increase the ability of the lungs, heart, blood, and blood vessels to deliver oxygen to the cells' door-

WHAT ABOUT FAT?

Body fat, except in small quantities, is the enemy. A pound of fat on your ribs slows you down much more than an extra pound of metal on your bike; the fat is living tissue, and it uses oxygen and nutrients that would otherwise be available to your muscles.

You can measure your body fat percentage by using special callipers which pinch your skin and measure the thickness of the fat layer underneath. Inexpensive versions of these callipers are now available.

Average adult males have about 20 per cent body fat; females run 2-3 per cent higher. Elite U.S. male cyclists usually have 7-10 per cent; women, 10-15 per cent. European pro racers have less fat than U.S. males—that's why you see their veins bulging.

WHAT ABOUT YOUR RECORDS?

What was your basal pulse last week? Exactly how much training did you do for that century last year?

There's no substitute for a training diary, and the time to start one is today. You don't have to be a serious athlete. Anyone who exercises will benefit from one. A written record tells what kind of training leads to what kind of performance providing a realistic gauge of how much work it takes to get back on track after a layoff.

A diary like this provides a unique record of your body's performance. Besides, no one else is going to keep one for you.

Specially published training diaries are available, but I still use a spiral-bound notebook, as I started doing during the Sixties. I record my mileage, how I felt, any alternative exercises, sick days, and flake days. Because I've been keeping the diary so long, I can see the effects of advancing age on my training I can go as fast, but I take longer to recover.

step but those systems will develop more than the cells will, and the cells themselves create the ultimate bottleneck.

When you pant like gangbusters and your pulse skyrockets, your body systems are trying to deliver more oxygen to the muscle cells. To some extent it is a futile effort, because the muscle cells can only consume so much oxygen at a time. However, making more oxygen available to the blood shortens and minimizes the inevitable lactic acid build-up. The skyrocketing pulse is also a useful way for you to determine your anaerobic threshold. Dr. Francesco Conconi, the trainer for World Hour Record Holder Francesco Moser, has used it to great advantage. When you're within your aerobic range, your pulse increases at about the rate your bike's speed increases. When you go anaerobic, the rate of pulse increase steepens drastically.

By the way, this explains why the blood doping engaged in by some 1984 U.S. Olympic cyclists may well have been a waste of time. As pointed out by Dr. James Dolan of Pennsylvania's Lock Haven University, all those cyclists did was to increase their blood volume, and they already had all they could use. Blood doping doesn't increase the muscle cells' ability to use oxygen, the true bottleneck.

Questions about aerobic capacity and performance improvement further complicate the unending debate about How Much Exercise Is Good for You. The training schedule in Chapter 2, which barely scratches the surface of bike riding ability, is enough to build aerobic capacity and more than sufficient to shoo away heart attacks.

But I believe you'll want to do more, because there are greater rewards to be had. It's fun to go fast, and it's delightful to feel your body get stronger week by week. You sleep better, your appetite matches your energy expenditure better, you wake up with more energy and carry it with you all day long, and feel better about your whole life.

Cycling isn't a weight-bearing sport, and the ranges of motion and primary muscles used are entirely different from standard weight bearing activities. The only other sport which even faintly resembles it is speed skating. The primary muscles are in the upper thigh muscles, the quadriceps, and in the bum—the gluteus maximus. The calf muscles —gastrocnemius and soleus—work some, too. Train regularly, and these muscles will become stronger, harder, and, depending on your hormones, bigger.

Because muscle training is so specific, you can't use cycling to train for another sport, except for general aerobic conditioning.

Moreover, because cycling trains muscles selectively and largely ignores their opposing muscles (i.e. the hamstrings which opposes the quadricep, and the shin muscles—tibialis anterior and peroneals—which oppose the calves), you can easily develop a severe imbalance in muscle strength and tightness. These opposed muscle pairs need to be matched in strength; if lopsided development strengthens one much more than the other, the results can be discomfort, susceptibility to injury, muscle tightness, and awkwardness.

I've experienced the classic cyclists' imbalance problems, of quads overpowering hamstrings, and calves overpowering shins. My hamstrings even tightened up in response. The results were a bit of constant nerve pain in one hamstring and calves so tight they wanted to point my toes down all the time.

A stretching programme described later in this chapter, cured me and restored some of the limberness of my youth. I also exercised and strengthened the hamstrings with weights on a Nautilus machine and with running.

My emphasis so far has been on long distance training, tempered with the assumption that your time for training is limited. Long rides develop the body's ability to burn fat rather than glucose, and form a pre-season base for later, more intense effort. Even a future velodrome sprint specialist needs this base.

Moreover, what I'm selling here is comfort. Feeling fresh—really fresh, with snap still left in your legs—after 80, 90, 100 miles. That's the pot of gold at the end of the long distance rainbow. I've been there, and it's absolutely wonderful, and well worth the effort.

If you hammer yourself on 15-mile rides, you'll always be tired and full of lactic acid at the end, and you won't ever feel that you can tackle longer training rides.

Also, the changes in your metabolism which result from long distance training have a beneficial knock-on effect on your stamina. You're off the bike most hours of the day, and this training strategy will benefit those hours more than impatient short rides.

What if you don't have the time for long distance training?

You could become a competitive bike racer! Sounds contradictory, but it's true. Most sanctioned races for entry-level riders are brutally short and fast typically 10 or 15 miles often around a one-mile course with four sharp corners. You need great bike handling skills and the ability to sprint out of 40 to 60 corners. You don't have time to burn any fat. And seriously, you can train quite effectively for these races with intense 20-mile training rides. Or, without racing or hurting quite so much in training, you can get in good cardiovascular shape without developing your fat-burning ability. In that respect, you'll be on equal footing with those people who run four miles per day. When you do go on a longer ride, take it especially easy. You won't know when you've run out of glycogen until it's too late.

Overtraining

Beware of overtraining.

I once conquered a personal Everest that did lasting damage to my cycling career: a 700-mile week. I did it, with 79 miles to spare, and then became hopelessly stale. For months afterward, there was no spring in my stride. What a mistake! I had built myself into terrific condition riding 400, even 500, miles per week, and if I'd held myself 'down' to that level, I would have built both strength and speed and continued to improve to the point where I could take a 700-mile week in stride.

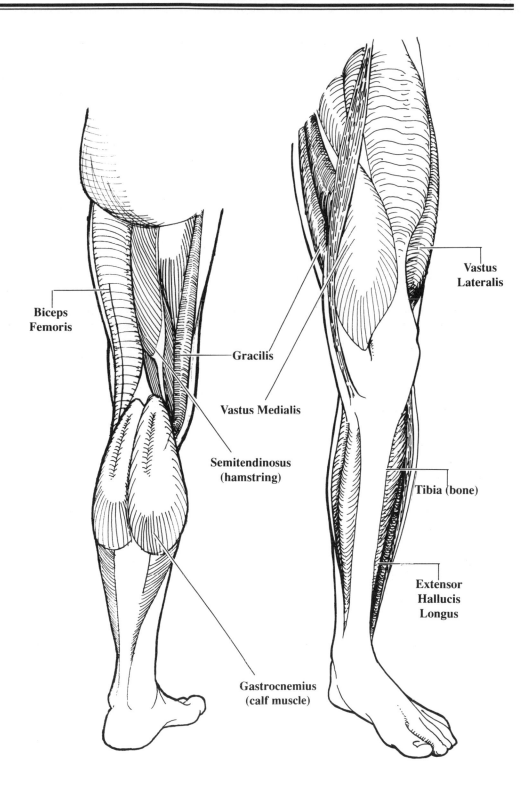

Biceps Femoris

Gracilis

Vastus Medialis

Semitendinosus (hamstring)

Gastrocnemius (calf muscle)

Vastus Lateralis

Tibia (bone)

Extensor Hallucis Longus

I had a case of training diary madness. Instead of trying to ride well, I made the numbers look great.

There are legions of athletes who make the overtraining mistake every day. A man I know ran 100 miles per week for a year, and ruined his health in the process. He failed to follow an important message: the amount of time spent with your nose on the grindstone does not have a linear relationship to success. And the reason for this is quite simple: working out tears your body down. Those muscle fibres you've been working are injured, and they need repair. Your liver needs days as long as two weeks after a super-long event to replenish its supply of glycogen. The metabolic slag present in your bloodstream and muscle tissues takes an extra day or two to disappear.

What rebuilds the body? Rest. For ordinary folks whose recuperation powers are modest, this sometimes dictates rest days with no exercise at all. A hard ride may require that the next day's work-out should be climbing into a soothing whirlpool bath.

As your condition improves, your recuperative powers also improve, and a hard ride does less damage to the system. You reach the point where you seldom need out-and-out rest days. Short days, yes that barn-burning century on Sunday may dictate easy five-mile spins on Monday and Tuesday, just to loosen up and stimulate blood circulation. And truly fit athletes relax in ways which are frightening to the rest of us; during the 'rest days' of the Tour de France, the riders typically go out for brisk 100-kilometre rides!

Don't let it be a badge of honour to push your body when it needs a break. If it asks for a rest, give it one.

The signs of overtraining are obvious. You're tired all the time, yet have trouble sleeping. When you get on the bike, you don't feel any snap in your legs. Your resistance to disease is low, and you're constantly on the verge of colds or flu. Muscle soreness doesn't go away with your easy days. Your riding gets slower.

If these signs aren't enough, you can test for overtraining by taking your basal pulse each morning. The second you wake up, before you yawn and stretch, before the cat jumps on your bed, before anything, slowly grasp the watch with one hand and your wrist or neck with the other, and take your pulse. Then stand up and take your pulse again. It will be faster. The morning after a hard work-out the difference between the two will be a few beats more than usual and that's a signal to take it easy, or to take a day off.

When you take your morning pulse, write it down. The accumulated information will help you understand the effect your training is having on you.

Undertraining

Undertraining has a surprising number of things in common with overtraining. For one thing, it slows you down. For another, you're more susceptible to injury. The overtrainer slowly wears out; the undertrainer doesn't toughen up enough. The result is abuse and injury when trying to ride a century with the big boys. Or the undertrainer becomes fog-headed, and has an accident.

Typical over/undertraining injuries include:

● Chronic soreness in the Achilles tendons. Very slow to heal; takes rest. You can usually keep riding without causing permanent damage, but the nagging pain will keep you from wanting to. Only a masochist can turn this into a serious injury, but it's been done.

● Handlebar palsy (hand numbness and/or loss of motor control). When you lean on your hands, you press on an important nerve that runs directly under the skin; pressure on that nerve shuts it off. It can take days to fully recover. Time off the bike is essential. If you persist in ignoring it, you can get permanent loss of nerve function. Heavily padded gloves usually solve the problem for most riders; a change in handlebar position or the rider's habitual posture on the bike may help by decreasing weight on the hands. When Spenco introduced the first heavily padded gloves several years ago, they found immediate acceptance among the riders in the RAAM marathon known as Race Across AMerica. After the race that year, the riders sat around talking to each other, marvelling that they still had enough motor control to touch their thumb to each of their fingers. They had all experienced partial hand paralysis in earlier years.

● Numb crotch. Like handlebar palsy in every respect. The same companies sell heavily padded seats and saddle covers.

● Knee soreness. Knees get sore from overuse or from biomechanical position problems. If your knees are chronically sore with modest mileage and no over ambitious efforts—or if they get sore even though you build mileage slowly—something is probably wrong with your basic position. Permanent damage may result. Get professional medical help. However, if your knees hurt only after you over extend yourself, don't panic. See if aspirin, a bag of ice, and two rest days solve the problem. Then review your training schedule.

The common knee problem is chondromalacia patella—a roughening of the backside of the kneecap. It occurs as a result of the kneecap travelling outside its matching groove in the thigh bone. This tracking problem can result from misalignment due to over pronation or cleat maladjustment—or even from a hip misalignment or previous trauma.

Perfectly aligned people seldom get chondromalacia, but those of us with flat feet, bow legs, and a propensity to over-pronate had better pay attention. Medical devices such as

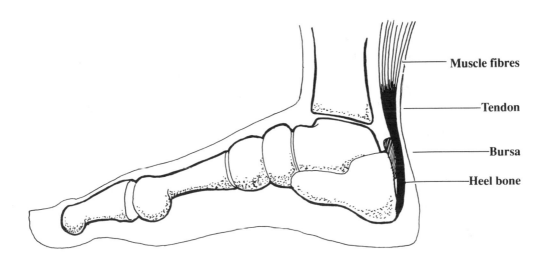

Muscle fibres

Tendon

Bursa

Heel bone

orthotics, and mechanical devices such as the Biopedal, can be used to correct bio-mechanical misalignment. Often these need to be combined with an exercise programme of leg extensions and leg curls, which strengthen and tighten the muscles surrounding the knee, and maintain the proper quad/ham strength ratio. When these muscles are tighter, they help hold the kneecap in proper alignment. In severe cases, a soft brace may correct the tracking for you while you strengthen your quads—and allow you to ride pain free.

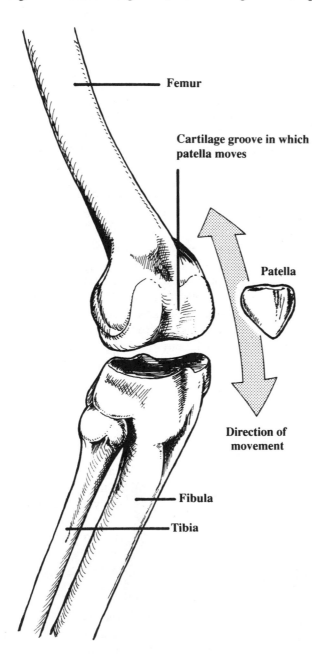

Femur

Cartilage groove in which patella moves

Patella

Direction of movement

Fibula

Tibia

If you have symptoms of chondromalacia, don't be a idiot and try to treat it yourself. The stakes are too high. Millions of people who love cycling, running, and other activities have been forced to give them up because they didn't understand how to treat the problems and badly injured themselves. Podiatrists, physical therapists, and certified athletic trainers are the medical specialists most likely to know how to help you.

Whenever you have an injury, pamper yourself. So many riders have made a minor injury major by continuing to train without treatment, or by continuing to ride that last 30 miles home the day the pain first appeared.

Avoid painkillers beyond the occasional aspirin; they just turn your body's warnings system off. And when you're out on a ride and you notice a new pain, spend a minute to examine it. Get off the bike, give the offending body part a few minutes' rest and massage,

FILLING IN THE GAPS

Okay, your parents both swam the Channel and you can only long-jump three feet. You'll never be a great sprinter.

Or you're a fine sprinter, but anything longer than three minutes generates a nagging pain you'd rather not feel.

One of bike racing's adages is 'train your weaknesses and race your strengths'. If you want to be much of a bike racer, follow this adage faithfully. It's tempting just to train your strengths. It feels better, and it's more fun and rewarding, in the short term. But it's not how the best cyclists got where they are.

Training one's weaknesses is an area where many competitive athletes, even national-class ones, fall down. I've known distance riders who were clearly stronger than the competition, but lost races and quit the sport because they had a mental image of themselves as non-sprinters and they never trained for sprinting. And many U.S. sprinters have never trained for the longer events or done well in them.

Competitive cyclists in the European tradition frown on such specialization. Many of the finest names in sprinting have also had some major road victories, and the best roadmen must, by necessity, learn to outsprint each other. You have to be a sprinter to win a six-day velodrome race, but you also have had to race a couple hours a day for six days! These cyclists mix sprinting and endurance abilities more than runners, football players, or almost any other athletes.

One year when the East German track racers came to the U.S. for training, they revealed the unglamorous secret behind their competitive success: all of them, in cluding the 200-metre specialists, trained long and hard on 100-mile jaunts into the hills surrounding Los Angeles.

and think about it. If riding home is going to make it worse, use your magic pain-relieving tool: your thumb. Get a ride in the sag wagon and save yourself.

Stretching

If cycling has a drawback as exercise, it's the lack of stretching. Because muscles naturally lighten up when you exercise them, and because you don't need much range of motion to ride a bike, a dedicated bike rider can find himself tightened up into a little ball. If you're not naturally limber and you don't compensate by stretching, this can cause some real problems. You can be so stiff that you have trouble climbing out of the back seat of a small car, or you can easily pull a muscle and injure yourself the day you decide to go running or play tennis with friends.

Stretching is no fun. It hurts and it reminds you how tight you are. To make matters worse, it has to be done often—preferably each day; a bare minimum of four times per week—and you're lucky if you can get through a decent stretching session in 15 minutes. Dedicated stretchers take twice that long. But there are some tricks that let you incorporate stretching into your routine daily activities.

The first thing to do is build a slant board. You need a scrap of wood such as half-inch plywood, large enough to stand on, and two scraps of two-by-four. Cut the two-by-four into wedge-shaped pieces. Use a 30-degree angle if you're naturally limber (that's the standard for professionals. Use 15 degrees if you're naturally tight. Nail or screw the

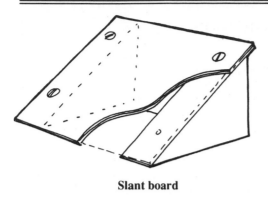

Slant board

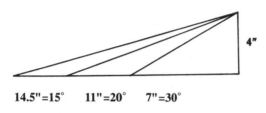

4"

14.5"=15°　　11"=20°　　7"=30°

wedges on to the edges of the plywood scraps, and you have a slant board.

Keep the slant board where you do routine tasks. I keep mine in the kitchen and stand on it each time I do the washing up. The ten minutes I spend doing the dishes thereby doubles as ten minutes stretching the calves and, to a lesser extent, the hamstrings —the two muscle groups which cyclists have the worst tightness problems with. This gentle, passive stretching won't make you a gymnast, but it's a good starting point.

The rest of your stretching exercises won't leave your hands free, but at least you can do them while you watch the news. Make sure you're isolating and stretching the particular muscle, not bending the rest of the body and cheating. Stretch to the point of tightness, not to the point of pain or dis-comfort. And do it slowly. Make it part of your daily routine—otherwise, it won't help.

Stretching produces better results more quickly if you use the contract/relax method. Put yourself in the stretched position, then, holding that position, contract the muscle you're trying to stretch.

Try to push the limb against the wall/table/floor which is constraining it. After about ten seconds of contraction, relax the muscle. Now you'll find it's more limber, and you can stretch it a bit more without discomfort. Repeat this once.

● Hamstring stretch. Finish stretching those nasty tight hamstrings by putting one foot up on a table. Hold your hips still, bend over, and try to touch your toes.This exercise is a natural for the contract-relax method. Just try to push the table through the floor with that outstretched leg. Don't forget to do the other leg, too!

● Quad stretch. Lie on your stomach and bend one knee, bringing your foot to your rear end and don't let that rear end stick up into the air while you do this. Reach behind you and grasp that ankle. Still not tight en-ough? Raise the thigh as far off the floor as you can. If your quads are so tight you can't reach your ankle in the first place, grab a towel wrapped around the ankle.

● Groin stretch. Sit on the floor and bring the soles of your feet together in front of

Groin stretch

Hamstring stretch

you. Try to lower your knees to the floor. Use the contract-relax method by holding your knees down with your elbows, and pushing up against the elbows.

When you relax, apply a steady pressure downward against your knees, and be sure not to bounce.

● Wall stretch. Stand two feet away from a wall, put your hands flat on the wall in front of you, and lean into the wall. This stretches your calves.

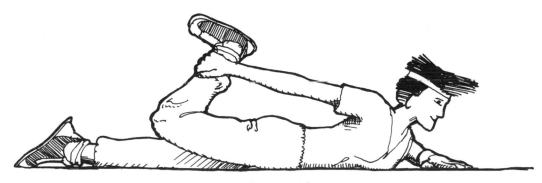

Quad stretch

If you want to add a simultaneous stretch to the pectoral muscles in your chest, do this exercise facing a corner instead of a flat wall.

There are countless other stretching exercises you can do; generally, they're different ways of stretching the same muscles addressed above. What's important is doing them regularly. A week off your bike won't set you back as much as a week without stretching.

Altitude

If your riding takes you to different parts of the country, you're bound to find out what difference altitude makes. If you live like most people in the UK at or near sea level and then decide to take your bikes to the Alps you can expect to get out of breath more quickly than you are used to. The solution is to restrict yourself to lower gears and slower speeds. Try to bully your way through a little thin air and altitude sickness will bite you with headaches and nausea. It takes about two weeks of living and riding at high altitude to enable most people to adjust and function normally.

You'd think that ability at altitude would give you more aerobic power, and speed on a bike at sea level. It doesn't. Acclimatizing to altitude increases the ability of the lungs to take in oxygen. But the usual limitation in oxygen consumption is in the muscle cells. Altitude training doesn't do a thing for them.

Wall stretch

Training by Heart Rate

The new generation of pulse monitors has made it practical to gear your training around your heart rate—certainly a more scientific method than training by feel. The pulse monitor helps you listen to your body, and it can give a very accurate picture of how the various levels of exertion feel.

The harder you ride, the faster your pulse. When you recover, your pulse drops. Pulse is such a reliable indicator of exercise work-load that it makes training simpler and more precise. Any rider with a possibility of medical problems should buy and use a pulse monitor. It's cheap insurance against accidentally exceeding your doctor's orders.

Riders who don't want another gadget to come between them and the beatific zen of cycling can nearly duplicate the effects of a pulse monitor, but it takes some work. You learn to take your pulse while on the bike, and do so

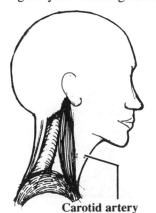

Carotid artery

regularly. Put one hand on your neck and grasp the carotid artery. Move the other hand towards the centre of the bars, so your weight on that hand won't make you steer to one side. Make sure you can see your watch. Take the pulse for five seconds and multiply by 12. (If you can't pedal while counting your pulse, how many balls can you juggle at once?) Pedal right up until the second before you start counting. Otherwise, your reading will be a false low. Obviously, you can only do this on a deserted, wide road. It's not hard to see why pulse monitors are getting popular!

If you don't have a pulse monitor, it's probably more practical to use your breathing rate as a guide to how hard you're working. When your breathing becomes laboured, you're somewhere near the maximum aerobic training rate.

Here are the traditional heart rate numbers to know about.

A conservative estimate of your maximum, never-exceed heart beats per minute rate, is 220 minus your age. For a 35-year-old, this is 185.

The maximum aerobic training rate, right at anaerobic threshold, is about 85 per cent of maximum rate, or 157 for the 35-year-old.

The minimum rate for good aerobic training is traditionally 70 per cent of the maximum rate, or 130 for the 35-year-old.

However, these numbers are gross over-simplifications. An older, sedentary person may go anaerobic at 50 per cent. An untrained individual may get good training at 70 per cent at the beginning of an exercise programme, and then need to go to 75 per cent after a month of training. And according to a recent study conducted by Pat Ennis, Mike Argientieri, and Linda Piper, a well-trained cyclist may need to exceed 85 per cent to get close to anaerobic threshold. Ennis and company tested ten trained cyclists for anaerobic threshold as measured by expired gases, work-load, and pulse monitoring and found that for four of them, good aerobic training began above 85 per cent. Five would be under-

SUGARING THE PILL

Here's the skinny on glucose, glycogen, and how to make them work for you. Glucose, stored in the muscles and flowing in the blood, is the fuel your muscles love the most, the stuff you want to teach them to do without, so they'll be content with fat.

Glucose comes from glycogen, and glycogen is stored in the liver. Glycogen is nothing more than a huge chain of glucose molecules. The glucose molecules are chewed off one at a time and thrust into the bloodstream so they can travel to the muscles and get used up.

For a reasonably well-trained athlete, the liver's glycogen supply lasts about two hours. If you're still out riding when it's exhausted, you feel the proverbial road kill.

That's the bonk, or as runners call it, the wall.

It normally takes the liver two days to completely replenish its glycogen supply, but research on marathon runners by the one noted expert, Dr. David Costill, indicates that under conditions of extreme glycogen depletion, it can take two weeks. Of course, you can help by eating and drinking carbohydrates—that's why stage racers eat while they ride. Bananas, rice cakes, carbohydrate drinks, and other such foods will provide a trickle of glucose during a ride. Eating during a ride, though, doesn't come naturally. It's another skill for you to practise.

training somewhat if they went by the standard guidelines. One rider, the youngest in the study, would be overtraining.

The Ennis study shows there's still no substitute for listening to your body. However, here are the standard rules of thumb about training pulse rate, just in case they apply to you. The pulse you target on your rides depends on your goals. To burn fat on a long ride, you need to be near the 70 per cent figure. To increase aerobic capacity, you need to try to stay quite close to 85 per cent. For interval training and speedwork, discussed in a later chapter, you try to pin the needle and hold it there. Then you relax and pedal easily until your pulse has dropped to 120—a fast idle for a healthy heart—and repeat the interval.

Muscle Fibre Types

You're probably familiar with the difference between fast twitch and slow twitch muscle fibres. Most humans have about half of each, plus or minus ten per cent. Slow twitch fibres, called red fibres because they can store so much myoglobin (oxygen-storing protein), have the endurance to perform over a long period of time, if enough oxygen is delivered to them. Fast twitch fibres are white, develop their peak tension in one-fifth of the time after stimulation and fatigue easily. They have superior anaerobic capability.

Both fast twitch and slow twitch muscle fibres can be trained for both slow aerobic and fast anaerobic work. So even the slowest endurance-oriented rider can make substantial improvements in his sprint, and even the fastest flash-in-the-pan rider can improve his endurance. However, you can't change the muscle fibres you were born with, and your competitive potential is, in that way, a product of heredity.

Heat, Cold, and Your Body Temperature

It's quite important to understand how your body regulates its temperature, and how the various systems involved in the process interact. At rest, your body metabolism generates about as much heat as a 150-watt light bulb. As you exercise, that heat generation increases—as much as tenfold, measured by calorie consumption.

The chemical reaction which changes fuel and oxygen into energy is only about one-third efficient. Engineers will recognize the laws of thermodynamics at work here. There is no getting around Mother Nature's limitations! For every calorie which turns the pedals, two heat up your body.

In winter, this extra heat is welcome. Even at springtime temperatures, the wind chill factor of bike riding has you wearing long sleeves and tights while runners are working on their suntans.

But in summer, you need to get rid of extra heat. Perspiration helps with this; moreover, the blood and circulatory system act as your body's internal cooling system. The blood brings heat generated within your muscles and core to the skin, and the skin acts as a radiator to carry the heat away. The blood vessels directly under the skin dilate to facilitate this process.

Cooling the body places a big demand on your circulatory system, which is already working to bring oxygen to the muscles. If body temperature is to stay within bounds, less blood must go to the muscles; you slow down.

If you haven't trained for hot weather and fly to the Costa del Sol for a quick summer cycling break and suddenly try to ride hard and fast, you will feel just terrible. You can seriously injure yourself and even bring on life-threatening heat stroke. This is doubly true if you dehydrate yourself, the subject of the following chapter.

A rider who has trained in cold weather is better off than a rider who hasn't trained at all. Even the cold weather rider trains his muscles to require less blood flow, leaving a bit more for cooling purposes. But training is justly famous for being specific, and the only really good way to train for hot weather is to train where it's hot. This develops your body's ability to simultaneously feed the muscles and bring blood out to the skin. Take it easy for your first few rides when the sun comes out—you don't develop this ability in a day. Some riders wear tights and jackets in warm weather for just this reason; when the dog days hit, their bodies are ready.

Be aware of increased core temperature if you are fortunate enough to spend time abroad riding in hot weather conditions. If you're riding hard without good cooling effect for example, climbing a hill, you will heat up beyond the regulation 98.6 degrees and it will feel bad. A temperature increase of two or three degrees is about the limit of comfort for most riders. Top athletes routinely finish races with core temperatures around 104 degrees, a point where headaches, great fatigue, and other warning signs start to flash. If you get those signs regularly, take your core temperature with a rectal thermometer after each ride. Those headaches are a mere two degrees away from the heat stroke territory of 106 degrees.

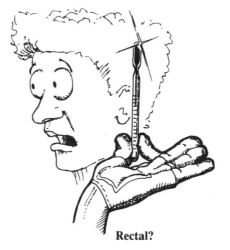

Rectal?

Several times, during the first few seconds after finishing a work-out, I've felt intense heat sweeping over my body, and almost fainted. The reason: the wind chill effect from riding was gone, but my core hadn't started to cool down, and I was still pumping heat from my core to my skin. I learned to go stand in front of a fan as soon as I got off the bike. And you're quite right, I had not warmed down properly.

The ultimate hot-weather danger is heat stroke. Increase core temperature enough—to about 106 degrees—and the body's natural thermostat, the hypothalamus, stops trying to cool the body down. The hypothalamus shuts down all sweating and reduces peripheral circulation. As a result, core temperature increases to as much as 110 degrees, consciousness is lost, and the brain is poached to death.

Signs of oncoming heat stroke are hard to miss. You'll be painfully overheated, with hot, red skin. But you may feel a chill—another sign of your thoroughly confused hypothalamus. Other signs are throbbing pressure in the head, deteriorating vision, breathing, and thinking. The cure: the victim is put in the shock position with feet elevated, and cooled down with ice and fluids applied to the skin. When the victim becomes alert, stop the ice and fluids—you don't want to cool him down too much.

INJURIES

Experienced riders know when to hold back a little bit on their training.

There's a good reason: your body strengthens itself unevenly in response to exercise, and one part of you is always more susceptible to injury than the others. Train too hard one year and you may get sore Achilles tendons—something you may need weeks to get rid of. The next year, your tendons are toughened up but your knees are quick to hurt. Then it's a system breakdown; by riding too long and hard, you lower your resistance to disease and get the flu.

The possibilities are endless, with sometimes comical consequences. On one famous occasion, the vaunted Eddy Merckx had to sit out the Tour de France because he had boils on his rear end.

There's always a weak link somewhere.

Cyclists get far fewer injuries than most other athletes, because cycling is non-weight-bearing, non-contact, and uses a limited range of motion. But don't ask for trouble.

If you're new to cycling, go easy and get to know what it feels like. If you're coming back after a lay-off, don't try to regain your former pinnacle of fitness in two weeks. Your training diary probably tells you of many instances where you tried that and just wound up sidelined. Mine certainly does.

In either case, *slowly* increase your effort level and duration.

Professional help is essential. Prevention: drink lots. Most people who have had heat stroke got dehydrated first; dehydration reduces your body's ability to rid itself of heat.

In winter, your circulation system still delivers core heat to the skin and extremities, but it has the ability to limit this heat, or even come close to shutting it off. As blood flows outward along your limbs, it can transfer heat to the blood returning to the core. Or the blood circulation can be shut down. Therefore, this heat is conserved, and the surface of your arm is allowed to get quite cold, even though blood still flows through the limb and supplies oxygen and glucose.

Your body will limit the heat supplied to the extremities in order to preserve, in order of importance, your brain temperature and your core temperature. The head gets full circulation no matter what, which is why hats are such a good idea.

THE MYTHICAL BUZZ

Endorphins are morphine derivatives naturally secreted by the body. Not long ago endorphins were blamed or credited for creating the 'runner's high' and the other pleasant feelings that went along with sustained aerobic exercise. In fact, sports medicine professionals were heard musing that athletes might develop a physical addiction to these endorphins, just like junkies and heroin. It would explain why runners go out on days when their knees hurt and it's sleeting cats and dogs.

However, endorphins aren't a factor in aerobic exercise. The only time you get a substantial endorphin secretion is during supreme emergencies.

Cycling at 19 mph or jogging at 9 mph does not produce significant endorphin secretions. If we feel good, it's probably because our blood, brain, and muscles are pumped full of fresh oxygen.

You've probably noticed that when you're exercising in cold weather, you may get cold hands and feet while your core is overheating and even sweating. The reason is an imperfection in the design of humans: when your peripheral blood vessels get cold, they constrict, going into a spasm. The only thing that will get them out of that spasm is externally applied heat, e.g. your hot bath after the ride. So there's the rub: what gets cold, stays cold. For this reason, I warm my hands and feet in front of the stove before I leave the house on a winter ride, and wear gloves and shoe covers. When hands and feet leave the house warm, they generally stay that way.

Not many cyclists venture out in weather that threatens frost-bite (actual freezing of body tissue). If you're one of the few who do, remember that frost-bite occurs after the period of feeling cold or tingling is long over. The only sign is that the extremity turns white with nose and cheeks usually the first to go. Cold weather riding is best done with a companion, so you can regularly check each other for frost-bite.

CHAPTER 5

Eating
and
Drinking

Contents

It's Always Time for a Snack

Eat before you're hungry, drink before you're thirsty

—Anonymous

You're in lovely countryside, a third of the way through your favourite Sunday ride, and feeling completely self-satisfied and comfortable. You're not hungry or thirsty but it's 2 pm. and time for a snack. You force down a banana and bottoms-up your water bottle. When you ride a bike you must make a habit of eating and drinking frequently, or you won't replenish yourself in time. The sensations of hunger and thirst come too late to do any good.

You don't feel thirsty, for example, until you've sweated away half a gallon of water! To get back to even you have to drink four bottles of water but you can't. Your stomach won't hold that much; it needs to receive the water a few swallows at a time in order to pass it on to the bloodstream. And by the time you're half a gallon of water down, your body is already feeling nasty side effects. Your blood plasma has reduced in volume, sometimes by more than a quarter, and thickened, hampering its ability to handle the simultaneous demands of cooling your body and feeding your muscles.

These effects begin at an early level. For most people, they're in full stride before the loss of four pints and the onset of thirst. The rule of thumb is that sweating away two per cent of your body weight is enough to impair performance. Two per cent, for a 150-pound rider, is three pints.

With the blood circulation hampered, nutrients and oxygen can't reach the muscles, and waste products can't get out of them. The efficiency of the body's natural cooling system is reduced because of the loss of so much coolant fluid. On a hot day, it's a set-up for heat stroke.

Similarly, hunger sets in only after you've largely depleted your glycogen reserves. Moreover, assuming that your riding speed stays the same, your perceived effort will be the same until those reserves are almost gone and then, abruptly, you'll feel hungry and fatigued. On rides of two hours or less, this doesn't much matter. But on longer, grander rides, unless you add some sugar and carbohydrates to stay fresh in those later miles, the dreaded bonk arrives.

If you do eat and drink properly as you ride, the resulting boost to your performance can be nearly unbelievable. No one has proved this better than the riders in the Race Across AMerica (RAAM) , who over the last five years have refined their diets from road-side cheeseburgers to highly sophisticated all-nutrients-included liquids. They never get dehydrated or bonk; instead, they sometimes ride their last 100 or 200 miles averaging 20 mph. If they can do that, you can ride 100 miles without bonking, even without special food.

Hydration

Your first priority is to drink enough water to stay hydrated. On a hot day, it's nearly impossible to stay even with your sweating. The most you can do is lessen the dehydration during the course of the ride. A conservative estimate of your warm weather sweating rate is five pints, or five pounds, per hour. On a particularly hot, muggy day, I recorded a water

HEAVY RIDERS

You've picked the right sport. The bike supports your weight and you can use more of your energy to go forward.

What if you want to shed a few pounds? Here are the grim facts: a pound of fat has 3,500 calories. To get rid of that, pedalling away 200 to 400 calories per hour, depending on your effort level, you have to ride about 9-17 hours—at least one week's work for one little pound.

There isn't anything that takes the place of reforming eating habits. That said, exercise is a vital adjunct to losing weight through dieting, and cycling is one of the best. It is something a heavy person can do comfortably provided you're set up correctly on the bike. You can enjoy where you're going, which adds an immediate reward to cycling. And regular exercise can actually decrease your appetite.

If you diet without exercising, your basal metabolism drops, making it harder for you to lose weight. Your body may shed muscle tissue instead of fat. Exercise pumps up the basal rate of your metabolism, helping you to burn more calories just sitting there.

By stressing your muscles, exercise ensures that your body will lose fat, not muscle.

The most important effect is motivational. When you're feeling stronger and riding well, you get ambitious and want to ride even better. Having the bike to look forward to makes you want to get in to the best shape you can.

Want to keep weight off? Don't go on a diet—change the one you've got. If you go on a diet, then in your mind, it's always temporary. Your old ways loom in your mind, and returning to them, or a variation of them, is a logical plan. Instead, you want to burn the bridges to your old ways. That will really keep the weight off.

loss of six pounds in 40 minutes! For these reasons, I generally drink up to three pints at home just before leaving on a long, hot ride.

In hot weather, it doesn't matter how little or how much visible perspiration you see on your skin. To put it at its most extreme if you go touring in the North African desert, you may never even notice any signs of sweat. It evaporates quickly. In humid air, you'll see lots of sweat, but you won't be able to cool off as well, and your core temperature will rise, provoking even more sweating. Don't fight nature. Everyone rides slower in hot weather or injures himself trying not to.

If you plan to take long summer rides in a hot dry climate, equip your bike with two of the new quart-size water bottles. Ideally, you'd empty both of them during a one-hour ride. There's no physiological reason to save water for later. Your body will go ahead and sweat water just as profligately whether or not you drink now or save those last swallows for later. The only reason to save water would be for the comfort of rinsing out your mouth regularly during the ride.

The colder water is, the better it tastes. It also helps cool your overheated body core and, surprisingly, is absorbed into the bloodstream more quickly. Put your water bottles in the freezer an hour before the ride. For a while at least, they'll be more pleasant.

You can get dehydrated over a period of several days and not notice it. The onset of poorer performance will be too gradual for you to correctly attribute it to the cause. To protect against this, weigh yourself every morning. Down a pound? Drink a pint.

Replenishing Sugar

When you ride, your precious blood and muscle stores of glucose drop. Consuming sugar can help or hinder. It all depends on how you do it.

The classic example of hindering is when you consume a heavily sugared drink minutes before starting an event.

According to research by Dr. David Costill, it only takes five to seven minutes for sugar to get from your mouth into your bloodstream. Once in the blood, it threatens an increase in blood sugar level beyond that which the body will tolerate. Your body responds by dumping insulin—which neutralizes sugar—into the bloodstream.

The insulin installs your newly ingested blood glucose in muscle cells, from where it cannot be removed. That would be fine if it put all the glucose in your quadriceps, but it doesn't give you that option. Your arm and back muscles thereby get well supplied with non-transferable glucose. Meanwhile, the blood sugar level is lower than before. And, to add insult to injury, insulin reduces your ability to use fat for fuel.

If you drink a sugary fluid one hour before an event, though, you'll benefit. An hour gives the blood levels of insulin and glucose time to become normal..

When you consume sugar during an event, Costill writes, the sugar goes directly to the working muscles and spares the precious muscle stores of glucose.

But how should you take in that sugar?

Chocolate bars are out—they're full of energy-robbing fat, and they take too long to digest. Fruit is a mixed blessing. It tastes good and satisfies hunger pangs, but its fibre sits in the stomach, possibly hindering water absorption. And you don't really get enough calories from a piece of fruit. On the other hand, a juicy pear is more appetizing than say, lukewarm dilute cola. You may wish to compromise science for the sake of taste, at least on days other than race day.

Sugared drinks, whether traditional drinks like colas or exercise fluid replacement drinks marketed to athletes, have always been controversial because of their high sugar content. The conventional wisdom is that sugar water in high concentration sits in your stomach. Neither the sugar nor the water can get into your bloodstream to benefit you. For these reasons, cycling writers have spent the last 15 years urging people to dilute those heavily sugared drinks by at least one, and up to three, parts water—particularly in hot weather. For do-it-yourselfers, a tablespoon of sugar in 12 ounces of water is a typical recommendation.

The reason I say conventional wisdom is that a new eyebrow-raising theory has appeared. Costill, whose earlier research had supported the low sugar recommendations, has conducted new studies which give different results. In these, drinks with up to 15 per cent sugar—Gatorade is 5 per cent; cola is 10 per cent—were readily absorbed into the bloodstream by cyclists exercising at 70 per cent effort.

Whether you take advantage of this new information to put honey in your water bottle is up to you. Experiment and see what works for you, giving yourself several trials to become acclimatised to the various drinks you try. If your personal experience coincides with the new findings, you'll benefit from the added sugar—it will help stave off the bonk. Hard riding uses 400 or more calories per hour. I don't think anyone could drink enough to

stay even with that calorie consumption. Try anything you can to get a sugar surge before the final sprint; sprint performance increases in proportion to sugar content, since glucose consumption in a sprint may be 40 times the normal rate. Remember, too, that there's still just as much water in the more heavily sugared solutions—so your dehydration prevention programme isn't compromised. Your choice!

Note the three kinds of sugar: glucose, fructose, and sucrose. Fructose, or fruit sugar, produces the smallest insulin reaction. Glucose produces the greatest. (But these findings, too, are adrift in the sea of new, contradictory studies.) Sucrose, table sugar, is a 50/50 mix of the two. Fructose can be purchased in powdered form, or you can buy apples, pears, and bananas. The worst news in this entire chapter concerns ice-cream. Any bike rider worth his double-butted tubing lives for ice-cream, and the whole point of riding is to justify the halfway stop for a big mound of the stuff. But almost half of ice-cream's calories are in the form of fat, and the mere act of digesting that fat—like fat from bars of chocolate, or fat from a roast beef dinner drains energy from your system. You can't draw on that fat energy until the following day's ride, after you've digested it.

So if your day's ride is well within your ability, pull into the ice-cream stand and fill the bilge tanks. But if you're pushing the envelope—more miles, faster, than you're used to—pull into the nearest greengrocers.

One sugar replenishment strategy that works well for me on a day-long ride is to stick to fruit early in the day. When only an hour or two remains and I'm starting to drag, a cola gives a big lift. Even if the caffeine in the cola doesn't help me burn fat, it stimulates my tired bones.

Electrolytes

Top research several years ago encouraged athletes and athletic drink manufacturers to add electrolytes (mainly sodium and potassium) to their drinks. The reasons made sense: when your body levels of these electrolytes go down, they impair every body function from the nervous system functioning to coordination of muscle contractions.

But the newer research shows otherwise. For example, your blood potassium level drops when you exercise. But it isn't lost in sweat; instead, it migrates from blood plasma into body tissues. It's harder to get at and measure, but it's still there.

Riders new to heat tend to sweat away more salt than heat-trained riders. If you're new to heat and your diet is exceptionally low in table salt, you may need a small dab of additional salt. The rest of us have more than we can use. In fact, after a day of riding, we've sweated away much more water than salt, and our salt level has increased not decreased.

Caffeine used to be popular for its alleged role in helping the muscles use fat instead of glucose. That belief has now been largely discredited. Sorry—we'd all hoped that a cup of coffee could have the same effect as an additional 1,000 training miles!

Alcohol

I'm no teetotaller, but alcohol is simply incompatible with aerobic exercise. It's a diuretic that dehydrates you by inhibiting a function of the hypothalamus, secretion of the hormone ADH. ADH's job is to increase water resorption in the kidneys; with ADH gone, the water passes on through. That other famous diuretic, caffeine, works completely differently; it

inhibits re-absorption of sodium. If the sodium molecule can't be reabsorbed into the kidneys, it's obliged to pass through, taking some water with it.

Most people need to pee after drinking a beer. Even though beer is mostly water, the alcohol in it means you wind up with less water in your system because of the peeing. After a long ride, it's a big mistake to reward yourself with several beers. Your body is craving water , and you're just going to dry it out even more. You'll feel fat and happy for an hour or two, but after that you'll need a drink. At the least, drink a glass of water for every glass of beer. And the diuretic effect of alcohol may also cause your body to lose copious quantities of potassium, and require potassium replenishment!

Alcohol's next sin is that it ties up your digestion. It demands immediate attention from your stomach and liver. These organs draw blood away from the muscles and skin, because they need energy from the bloodstream to process the alcohol. And then, with agonizing slowness, they process that alcohol into fat—which you can't draw on for muscle energy until the following day. Keep your alcohol consumption modest and compensate for the effects of it by drinking more water than usual, and by having some food in your system to minimize the buzz that hampers your judgment and motor skills on the bike.

The Training Table

The day-in, day-out diet that will keep you going the fastest is high in complex carbohydrates, low in fat, and moderate in protein.

Fat slows you down while you digest it. Excess protein can slow you down, too. Exercising does not significantly increase your need for protein, so extra miles shouldn't translate into extra hamburgers. Protein is difficult and energy-absorbing to digest; processing protein requires extra water—possibly causing dehydration. And excess protein, which most of us eat lots of, cannot be stored. Instead it is laboriously converted into fat. For that matter, excess carbohydrate is converted into fat, too. Overeating is overeating.

The last meal before your big cycling event is important, but the eating patterns you've established before then are even more important. They'll determine how much glucose you've stored, how much fat and protein you're still trying to digest, and how busy your bowel is.

Now let's translate that into specific foods. For starters, you'll ride faster, feel better, and live longer if your diet includes the four basic food groups each day: milk/dairy products, meat/poultry/fish/eggs, bread/pasta/grains, and vegetables/fruits.

Eat moderate quantities of protein. Meat eaters needn't worry; they automatically get enough. Vegetarians must make a point of seeking out protein sources such as eggs (one per day; those egg yolks have too much cholesterol for you to eat more than that), milk, peanut butter—but watch its fat content, and tofu. Most vegetable protein is incomplete—it doesn't have all the amino acids. That's why the eggs and milk are important.

When you're riding actively, it's best to take your extra calorie needs with additional food from each of the four categories. You can enjoy pasta, non-fried potatoes, breads (all whole-grain unless you fall into the ultramarathon category), fruit, and vegetables.

Don't be a fanatic about avoiding fat. You need some. If you go to an extremely low-fat diet, you may even hinder the ability to use fat for fuel—that ability you've been cultivating in your training. However, note that fat ingested doesn't provide you with energy. There's a difference between muscle fat and general body fat.

The meals before the ride shouldn't be exotic. No experimenting with spices the night before, and no big lumps of protein, either—a nice pasta dinner is about the best you can do. Cut down on your fibre, too. This is one time you don't want fibre in your system. Milk is a poor breakfast beverage. For these reasons, pancakes make a good pre-ride breakfast; whole-grain fibrous cereal with milk isn't so good. Eggs are the worst possible breakfast for maximum ride performance, even though protein in the morning is normally good for you. Continental racers traditionally have rice cakes, biscuits, dried fruits and fruit tarts, and brown sugar. Good stuff!

Don't eat within one hour of starting time, or you'll depress your blood sugar level with an insulin reaction. (For most people, the butterflies-in-stomach factor enforces a two- or three-hour rule anyway.) And avoid sugar or food for 45 minutes after the ride begins.

You may be tempted to try carbohydrate loading—the programme where you temporarily increase your muscles' appetite for stored glucose by utterly exhausting them a week before the big event, teasing them with a couple of days of low-carbo diet, and then spending the last few days pouring on the pasta.

I counsel against carbohydrate loading. It doesn't always make you ride faster, it's easy to screw up, and people have observed negative side effects, including overall tightness, bloody urine, and even cardiac abnormalities that could lead to heart attack. A more prudent course is to have a nice pasta dinner the night before and enjoy those bananas and energy drinks during the ride.

Very high performance riders—ultramarathonists, racers training 500 miles per week— have special considerations. The sheer quantity of calories they need to consume is so

great that they have to be careful about ingesting too much fibre. Someone eating 6,000 calories per day from whole-grain breads and pastas will process so much fibre that he'll become a human fertilizer factory. And bloat himself trying to eat enough calories.

For these reasons, liquid carbohydrates and liquid all-nutrient foods are becoming more popular. They've come a long way from the evil stuff you used to stir into milk. The difference in bulk-per-calorie between liquid foods and, say, pasta, makes it much easier for the mega-athlete to get the food he needs. Even for a 100-mile-per-day rider it is often not possible to get enough calories with pasta, and that rider's glycogen stores will drop from day to day. Liquid carbohydrates allow sustained output at that level with barely any glycogen depletion from day to day!

The Long and Winding Road

Contents

Touring and Training
'Train, don't strain.'

Many cyclists are drawn to the challenge of a long ride. It might be an organized century with a patch and the click of a stopwatch as reward for riding 100 miles. Or it might be a private expedition to grandma's house just a few miles away, where the reward is a cup of tea and a cake.

Other cyclists prefer touring. Some like to go on inn-to-inn tours, and enjoy some brisk miles in between gourmet meals each day. (If you find a silver tandem in the barn where you park your bike, you'll find my wife and I inside by the fire.) Or self-contained touring, with a sleeping bag, tent, and primus stove, can feel particularly rewarding.

Long rides and touring can be done comfortably, with little or no strain. If you feel energetic, you'll naturally push the pace a bit and develop a strong cruise speed. But there is no need for anaerobic agony. This chapter is about training without strain, about feeling strong all day without hurting. Most of the work-outs will feel like long, brisk walks.

I'm combining the training techniques for touring (any ride that takes two or more days, with an overnight stay away from home) with training techniques for metric centuries, centuries, and other ambitious one-day rides. Hard-charging century riders will want to make use of the racing techniques in the following chapter. But I combine long one-day rides with touring to make a point: the pace is your own option. A long ride, even 100 miles, doesn't have to be arduous—if you're prepared for it.

The century is often called the cyclist's answer to the 26-mile marathon. But what a difference in wear and tear on the participant! Anyone who runs a marathon takes weeks to recover; with proper training, you can ride a century and feel very few side effects the following day.

A cycle tourist is fit in different ways than a racer, just as a backpacker's fitness is different from that of a distance runner. (If you've ever tried to stay up with a good backpacker, you know how brisk a long walk can be!) The cycle tourist, even the tourist who never strains, will be an incredibly fit athlete, with a fine cardiovascular system and low resting pulse.

In some ways, a tourist may be more fit than a racer who rides short criteriums. The racer is much faster, but his training concentrates on sprinting so much that his endurance is gone after an hour or two; a tourist's endurance is just starting to show its stuff after three hours. If you train for distance here are some ways you will differ from racers:

● You'll ride long, steady miles. If a racer's longest race is 20 miles, he may not bother.

● You'll always shift fluently, to keep your cadence and effort level constant throughout changing conditions. This is doubly true when touring with panniers. A rider on an unladen bike can get away with grinding up hills, but it's a knee-busting exercise in futility on a loaded bike.

Usually, the racer shifts just like you. But there will be times when a sudden sprint develops, and he won't have the time to shift. He'll have to jump in whatever gear he's in—low or high one.

● Your training is a steady effort at a comfortable level somewhere below aerobic maximum. About 40 per cent of the racer's training is out of the comfort zone, in fast jumps and sprints.

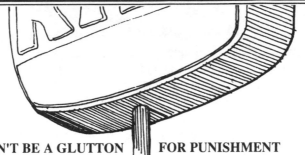

DON'T BE A GLUTTON FOR PUNISHMENT

Bicycle touring should be a string of picnics at refreshing swimming holes, stops at quaint inns and camping in lakeside pine forests, meandering on sunny country roads, fine evening meals, photography, and local lore. But all too often a tour turns into one endless bike ride.

I'm still baffled by the cycle tourists who persist in riding on congested four-lane A-roads, stay in anonymous motels and commercial campsites designed for camper vans and never see any sights more exotic than an Asda or Tesco car park. The situation is at its worst in my native America but with the relentless urbanisation of Europe, the same can apply here as well.

The solution is to plan ahead. Do some homework so you do the right things to have fun. Spend an hour in the library and read about the local history and culture of the area you're going to. Be outgoing, or bring along a friend who is. Make the sights you see, and the people you meet, come alive—you'll enjoy the trip more for it.

● How you climb hills is a matter of personal preference. How the racer climbs is dictated by the race, and by his strategy for doing well in that race.

● During your long rides, you practise eating and drinking on the bike. Again, the racer will only do that if his race distances warrant it.

● When you train with friends, your riding style is accommodating to them. The racer challenges his companions, it's part of training.

● You fine-tune the position on your bike for comfort. The racer fine-tunes for aerodynamics and handling.

Metric Century

The fitness base given in Chapter 2 is a four-week programme building up to 74 miles per week, with a longest day of 35 miles. That training schedule enables you to complete a metric century comfortably, if not quickly. You'd probably need a rest stop, and if you wanted to save yourself some fatigue, you'd give yourself a leg massage.

The next goal will be training for a brisk, comfortable metric 62-mile century, or a multi-day tour of 40 miles per day. (No, 40 miles per day isn't very macho. The point is to feel absolutely comfortable on those tours.) Full centuries and fast centuries follow later in the chapter.

The training schedule assumes you're still pressed for time during the week, but in the name of athletic ambition, squeeze in two midweek work-outs instead of one. You still ride both Saturday and Sunday, so you're now riding four times per week.

As mileage increases, a new consideration emerges: changes in distance must be very gradual. Big jumps from week to week were possible in the work-out schedule for a fitness base because the start was at a fairly easy level. Now, however, you'll be pushing closer to your true capacity. There are fewer rest days, more days when you cut your sleep short to wake up and ride, and more effort for your body to get used to.

These mileages are still modest, and you may feel impatient to get up to greater distances. But take the time to do the full schedule, and save yourself the agony of injury, illness, or that listless feeling from overtraining. A sensible rule of thumb is to increase your mileage no more than five to ten per cent every other week.

Here's the schedule:

Weeks 5 and 6—total, 88 miles

Sunday, 25 miles, easy twiddle—low gears and spin

Tuesday, 14 miles, maintain brisk pace in medium gears after short warm-up

Thursday, 14 miles, like Tuesday

Saturday, 35 miles. Five-mile warm-up, 20 miles maintaining stiff, even tempo, ten-mile warm-down.

Weeks 5 and 6 are exactly the same. It's a good idea to give yourself two weeks to adjust to the increase in days ridden and in total weekly mileage. Feel free to rearrange them and mix up the routes for variety's sake, but keep the total mileage constant.

I've stuck with a hard ride on Saturday followed by an easy Sunday. It's best to have a light ride, rather than a rest day, on the day after your hard ride. The light ride loosens you up. Of course, if you've really overcooked yourself, you'll need a day off.

Saturday's stiff, even tempo is your self-administered, self-correcting test to see if you

DEFINING PACE

How fast is 'naturally brisk'?

Cycling is so rich in technical information and numbers that many people are surprised by coaches describing work-outs in terms of how you're supposed to feel. Athletes who are used to work-outs specifying '6:45 pace', or 'four half-miles at 2:35 each', can find this frustrating.

But those terms simply don't work in cycling. First of all, the precise terms of running and swimming are borrowed from the track and pool, whereas you cycle on the open road where even the gentlest winds and hills make a big difference. Even when track racers work out on a velodrome, they don't do many timed efforts. Except for the occasional 200-metre flying-start time trial, most track work-outs don't involve the stopwatch.

Thus, I can't tell you 'maintain XX mph.' Any given speed could be relatively easy on a calm day in East Anglia, impossible on a windy day in East Anglia, or a laughing matter in the hills of the Lake District. Moreover, riders vary in ability, and the thing to do is ride *your* work-out—not someone else's.

Prescribing effort levels by assigning pulse rates is also imprecise, as appropriate pulse rates vary greatly from rider to rider, and no known rule of thumb can encompass all of these variations.

So we have to agree on descriptions. Even these are approximate, because people are different, and because individual speeds vary dramatically during a single season. In the early season when you're not in your best condition, the last two, and possibly the last three, of the categories below will run together. Here goes:

Easy twiddle: Emphasize a brisk cadence, high 90s or low 100s. Use a gear in the low 60s, rapidly downshifting for the slightest uphill. It shouldn't feel like work, or like you're pushing on the pedals. If you reach 20 mph, you're working much too hard.

Brisk pace, medium gears: You'll use about the same cadence. For a fairly strong rider in midseason, this will mean a flatland gear from 70 to 75 inches and a cruising speed of about 20 mph.

Stiff tempo: Now you're close to your aerobic threshold, but still taking care not to exceed it. A strong rider will use a flatland gear around 80 inches and a cruising speed in the 20s.

Maximum aerobic speed: You're right on your aerobic threshold. For most fairly strong riders, a gear around 85 inches puts you there.

know how fast you can comfortably pedal for a sustained period of time. If you find yourself running out of suds and slowing down, then you tried to maintain too high an effort. If you never feel winded, then you didn't try hard enough. The assignment is as much psychological and technical as it is physical. You have to learn what a stiff effort level feels like, and how to shift to stay at that level. The midweek work-outs are brisk, on the theory that you'll be rested up, and in a hurry to complete them and get on with the rest of your day.

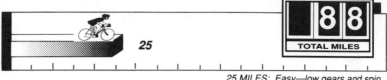

25 MILES: Easy—low gears and spin

WEEK 5

This week has the first hard bite: Saturday's 20 miles at a stiff, even tempo. Slow down if you run out of energy, speed up if you don't feel winded. Find out what a stiff effort is for *you*.

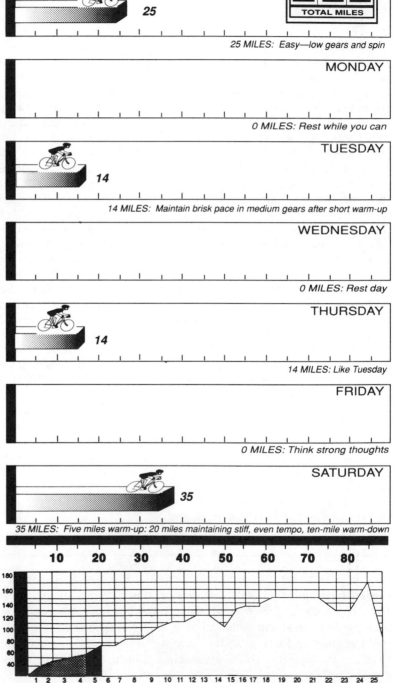

MONDAY

0 MILES: Rest while you can

TUESDAY

14 MILES: Maintain brisk pace in medium gears after short warm-up

WEDNESDAY

0 MILES: Rest day

THURSDAY

14 MILES: Like Tuesday

FRIDAY

0 MILES: Think strong thoughts

SATURDAY

35 MILES: Five miles warm-up: 20 miles maintaining stiff, even tempo, ten-mile warm-down

TOTAL FITNESS BASE MILES 334

25 MILES: Easy—low gears and spin

WEEK 6

Same as week 5.
It takes time to get
used to more
frequent rides and
increased miles.
Pace Saturday's
stiff effort
carefully.

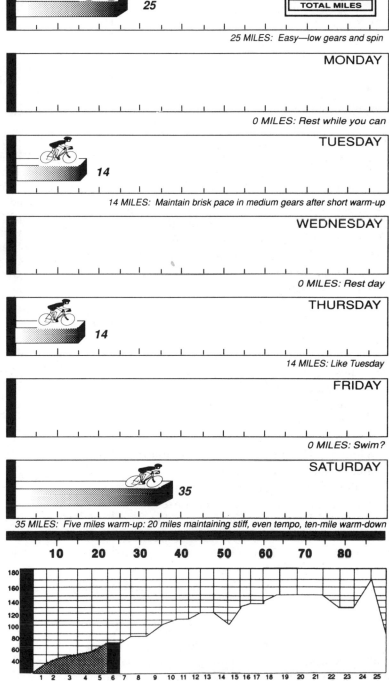

25

MONDAY

0 MILES: Rest while you can

TUESDAY

14

14 MILES: Maintain brisk pace in medium gears after short warm-up

WEDNESDAY

0 MILES: Rest day

THURSDAY

14

14 MILES: Like Tuesday

FRIDAY

0 MILES: Swim?

SATURDAY

35

35 MILES: Five miles warm-up: 20 miles maintaining stiff, even tempo, ten-mile warm-down

TOTAL
FITNESS BASE
MILES
422

Weeks 7 and 8—total, 93 miles each
   Sunday, 25 miles, easy twiddle
   Tuesday, 14 miles, brisk pace
   Thursday, 14 miles, brisk pace
   Saturday, 40 miles.

Week 7: Five-mile warm-up—25 miles of brisk pace, ten-mile warm-down.

Week 8: Five-mile warm-up, five miles of medium-brisk pace, two miles hard (maximum aerobic speed), two easy, two hard, two easy, two hard, 20 miles tapering off to long warm-down and finish.

The weekly mileage remains the same, but the second week's long ride works you a bit harder. The two-mile-long surges test your aerobic capacity, teach you where your anaerobic threshold is, and help you ride faster. Slowing down after two miles to an easy pace is very important so that you don't tire out and go stale; instead, you recover fully so you go hard during the next surge.

In real life, even riders with electronic speedometers have trouble carving their rides into neat two-mile segments. Look at the map before you go and round these segments off to the nearest village or other obvious landmark.

Week 9—total, 100 miles
   Sunday, 27 miles, easy twiddle
   Tuesday, 14 miles, brisk pace
   Thursday, 14 miles, brisk pace
   Saturday, 45 miles. Five-mile warm-up, 25 miles brisk, 15-mile warm-down.

With these work-outs, you've gradually built yourself a fine fitness base and raised your weekly mileage to three digits. Now if you go back to that metric century (after a week of tapering down with easy rides), you'll be much stronger than the first time around. Allow ten miles to warm up, then go hard for 45 miles. Your body will slow down naturally for the warm-down!

SHAPING UP FOR A TOUR

You'll sometimes hear a friend say, 'I'm going on a bike tour, but I don't have time to get in shape. I'll get in shape on the tour. I'll just ride slowly the first few days.' Silly. First of all, it's no fun to ride slowly if you don't feel like riding at all. If you are unprepared, by the second day you've got no glycogen and your muscles are sore. Willpower won't overcome an empty liver. You really can't go at all! (You might not notice the effect of this empty liver syndrome during one-day work-outs, so it'll hit you by surprise right when you want to have fun.)

Second, who wants to be sore and stiff on holiday? You're bound to resent the fact that other people on their bikes are lively and full of energy, while you just want to curl up with a hot water bottle and good book.

Third, even the most luxurious evening at a pub isn't as good a way to relax after a work-out as your own home. You recover better in your own surroundings, where you've made a thousand small accommodations to your own comfort.

Everyone makes first-time mistakes; they cause less anxiety when you make them training in the comfort of familiar surroundings.

Finally, a tired, sore rider isn't a safe rider. You want a break, not an accident. Some commercial touring companies offer short tours for absolute beginners.

English Century

For the English century of 100 miles, or for day-in, day-out touring of 50 miles, you need endurance, and lots of it; no fun getting the bonk with 25 miles to go. Accordingly, work-out distance is increased and the effort level cut back.

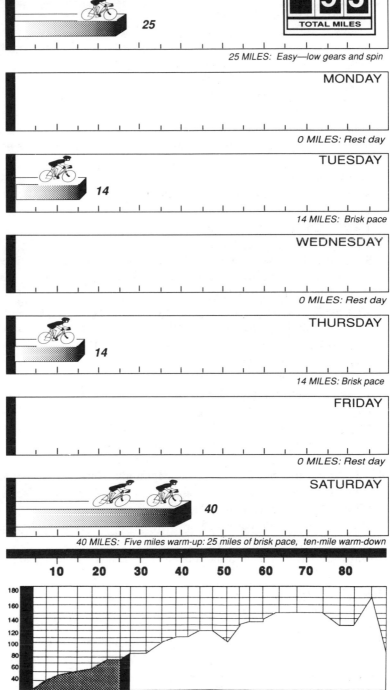

93 TOTAL MILES

25

25 MILES: Easy—low gears and spin

WEEK 7

Now you ride
at a brisk pace
more often,
and for longer
distances.
Be sure
to complete
warm downs.

MONDAY

0 MILES: Rest day

TUESDAY

14

14 MILES: Brisk pace

WEDNESDAY

0 MILES: Rest day

THURSDAY

14

14 MILES: Brisk pace

FRIDAY

0 MILES: Rest day

SATURDAY

40

40 MILES: Five miles warm-up: 25 miles of brisk pace, ten-mile warm-down

10   20   30   40   50   60   70   80

**TOTAL
FITNESS BASE
MILES
515**

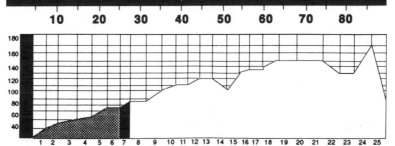

Weeks 10 and 11—total, 110 miles
    Sunday, 25 miles, easy twiddle
    Tuesday, 15 miles, brisk pace
    Thursday, 15 miles, brisk pace
    Saturday, 55 miles. Five-mile warm-up, 40 miles brisk, ten-mile warm-down.
    These two weeks are the same.
Weeks 12 and 13—total, 120 miles
    Sunday, 30 miles, easy twiddle
    Tuesday, 15 miles, brisk pace
    Thursday, 15 miles, brisk pace
    Saturday, 60 miles. Ten-mile warm-up, 40 miles brisk, ten-mile warm-down
    Again, these two weeks are the same. But now watch:
Week 14—total, 100 miles
    Sunday, 25 miles, mostly easy twiddle, with one two-mile stretch at maximum aerobic
speed
    Tuesday, 15 miles, brisk pace
    Thursday, 15 miles, brisk pace
    Saturday, 45 miles. Ten-mile warm-up, 20 miles divided into five sets of four miles per
set. Each set contains two miles at maximum aerobic speed, two recovering at easy
twiddle. Fifteen-mile warm-down.
    This week's mileage has been cut by 20 miles to toss in more high-effort riding. This is
a strategy to build aerobic capacity and ability to perform well in climbs, staying with fast-
moving groups, etc. It should make you feel more spry during the next two weeks:
    Weeks 15 and 16—total, 135 miles
    Sunday, 30 miles, easy twiddle
    Tuesday, 15 miles, brisk pace
    Thursday, 15 miles, brisk pace
    Saturday, 75 miles. Ten-mile warm-up, 55 miles brisk, ten-mile warm-down.
    Now you're ready to complete a century, almost easily. After two 75-mile work-outs,
your body will oblige you and complete the extra 25. It's a big jump—25 miles at the end
of the ride are tougher than 25 at the beginning—but you've methodically built up to it.
Warm up with ten slow miles, massage your legs and eat lots of fruit at the lunch stop, and
you'll ride 100 miles without undue strain.
    The last set of work-out schedules will speed up a century, or make it effortless to tour
about 65 miles per day.
    Many tourists go much farther than 65 miles each day, and you may wonder why such a
low ceiling. The answer: touring is drudgery if you spend too much time riding and too
little time enjoying yourself off the bike. And more mileage won't make you more fit—65
miles is all the day-in, day-out exercising most bodies can utilize. If you're looking for the
next level of accomplishment in cycling, it isn't to be found in ruining a holiday. Instead,
look to racing, double centuries, or even ultramarathon events.
    The last set of work-out schedules include another weekday morning ride. Now you
only get to sleep in two days a week.
    These schedules still assume your mid-week rides are limited to one rushed morning

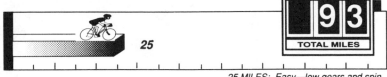

93 TOTAL MILES

25

25 MILES: Easy—low gears and spin

WEEK 8

Two miles hard at maximum aerobic speed. It's important to alternate with 2 miles easy for full recovery. Use obvious landmarks like villages and crossroads to pace out the stages.

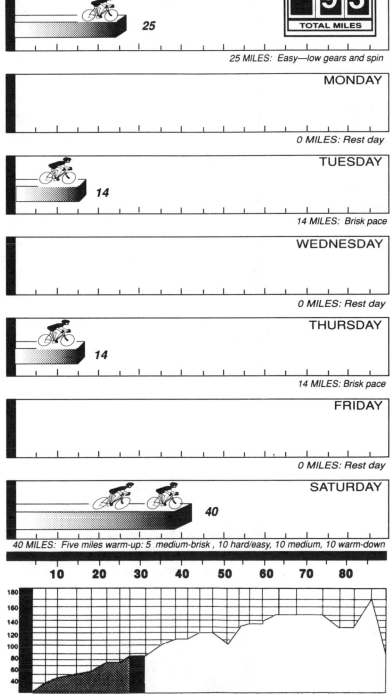

MONDAY

0 MILES: Rest day

TUESDAY

14

14 MILES: Brisk pace

WEDNESDAY

0 MILES: Rest day

THURSDAY

14

14 MILES: Brisk pace

FRIDAY

0 MILES: Rest day

SATURDAY

40

40 MILES: Five miles warm-up: 5 medium-brisk , 10 hard/easy, 10 medium, 10 warm-down

TOTAL
FITNESS BASE
MILES
608

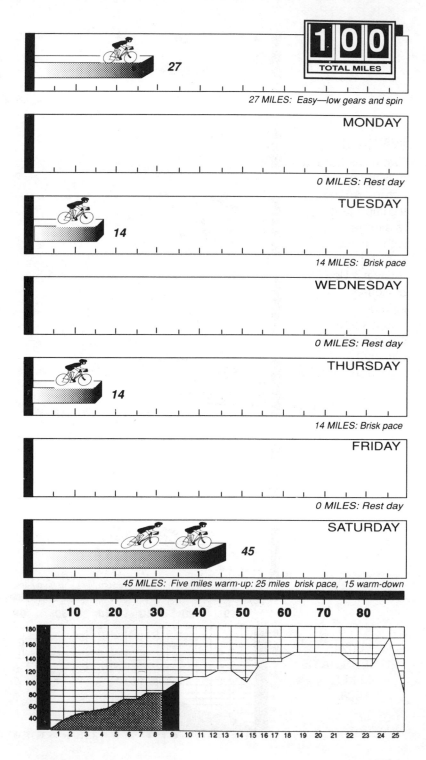

100 TOTAL MILES

27

27 MILES: Easy—low gears and spin

WEEK 9

The first
100-mile week!
After this you'll
be able to do
a 62-mile metric
century at
a good pace.

MONDAY

0 MILES: Rest day

TUESDAY

14

14 MILES: Brisk pace

WEDNESDAY

0 MILES: Rest day

THURSDAY

14

14 MILES: Brisk pace

FRIDAY

0 MILES: Rest day

SATURDAY

45

45 MILES: Five miles warm-up: 25 miles brisk pace, 15 warm-down

10   20   30   40   50   60   70   80

TOTAL
FITNESS BASE
MILES
708

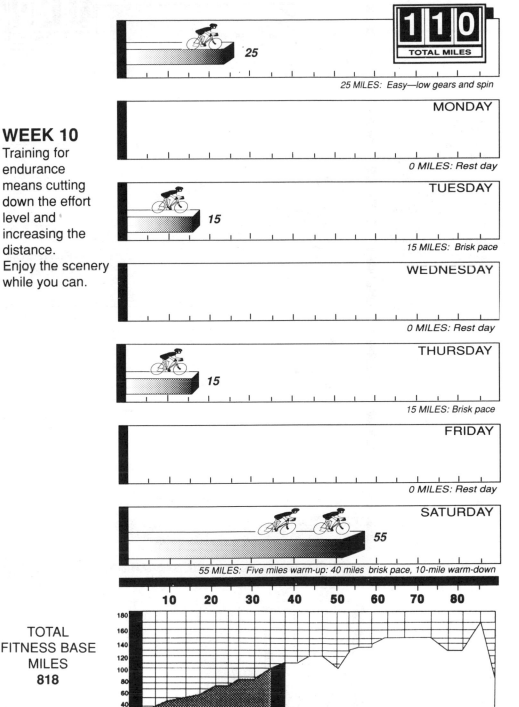

110 TOTAL MILES

25

25 MILES: Easy—low gears and spin

MONDAY

0 MILES: Rest day

WEEK 10

Training for
endurance
means cutting
down the effort
level and
increasing the
distance.
Enjoy the scenery
while you can.

TUESDAY

15

15 MILES: Brisk pace

WEDNESDAY

0 MILES: Rest day

THURSDAY

15

15 MILES: Brisk pace

FRIDAY

0 MILES: Rest day

SATURDAY

55

55 MILES: Five miles warm-up: 40 miles brisk pace, 10-mile warm-down

10 20 30 40 50 60 70 80

TOTAL
FITNESS BASE
MILES
818

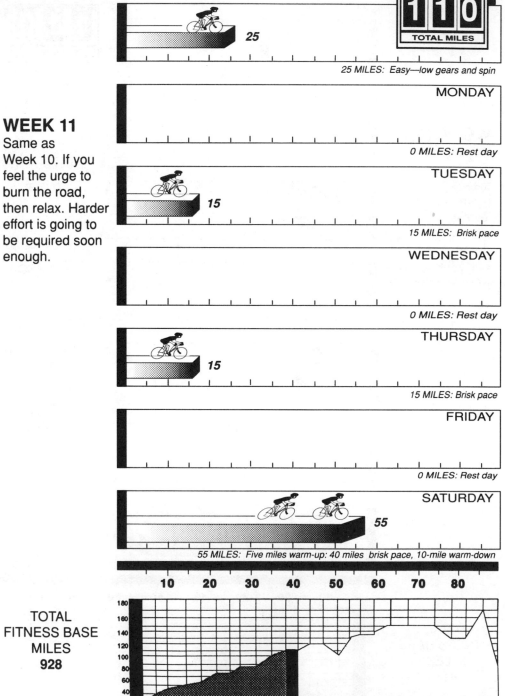

110 TOTAL MILES

25

25 MILES: Easy—low gears and spin

MONDAY

0 MILES: Rest day

WEEK 11

Same as Week 10. If you feel the urge to burn the road, then relax. Harder effort is going to be required soon enough.

TUESDAY

15

15 MILES: Brisk pace

WEDNESDAY

0 MILES: Rest day

THURSDAY

15

15 MILES: Brisk pace

FRIDAY

0 MILES: Rest day

SATURDAY

55

55 MILES: Five miles warm-up: 40 miles brisk pace, 10-mile warm-down

10 20 30 40 50 60 70 80

TOTAL FITNESS BASE MILES 928

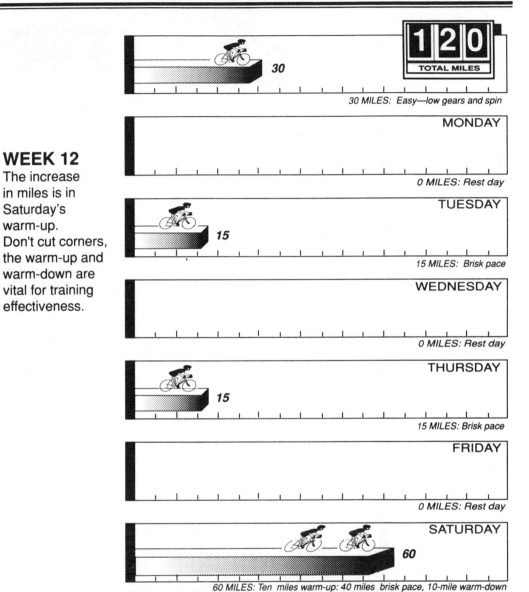

120 TOTAL MILES

30

30 MILES: Easy—low gears and spin

MONDAY

0 MILES: Rest day

WEEK 12

The increase in miles is in Saturday's warm-up. Don't cut corners, the warm-up and warm-down are vital for training effectiveness.

TUESDAY

15

15 MILES: Brisk pace

WEDNESDAY

0 MILES: Rest day

THURSDAY

15

15 MILES: Brisk pace

FRIDAY

0 MILES: Rest day

SATURDAY

60

60 MILES: Ten miles warm-up: 40 miles brisk pace, 10-mile warm-down

10   20   30   40   50   60   70   80

TOTAL FITNESS BASE MILES **1048**

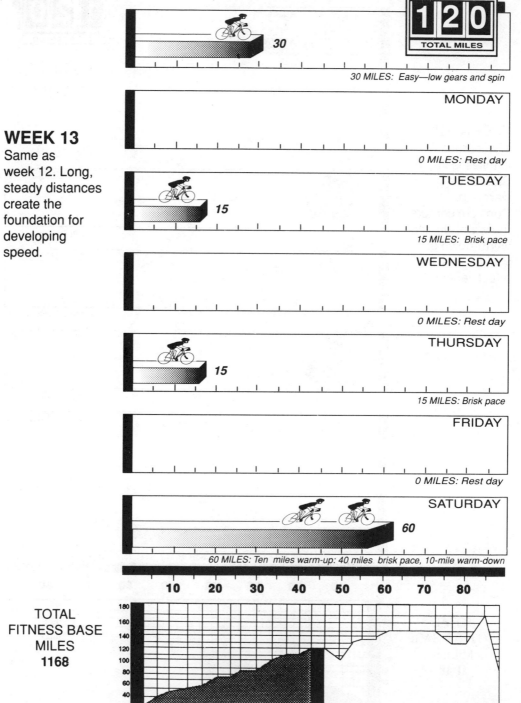

1 2 0
TOTAL MILES

30

30 MILES: Easy—low gears and spin

MONDAY

0 MILES: Rest day

WEEK 13
Same as week 12. Long, steady distances create the foundation for developing speed.

TUESDAY

15

15 MILES: Brisk pace

WEDNESDAY

0 MILES: Rest day

THURSDAY

15

15 MILES: Brisk pace

FRIDAY

0 MILES: Rest day

SATURDAY

60

60 MILES: Ten miles warm-up: 40 miles brisk pace, 10-mile warm-down

10   20   30   40   50   60   70   80

TOTAL
FITNESS BASE
MILES
1168

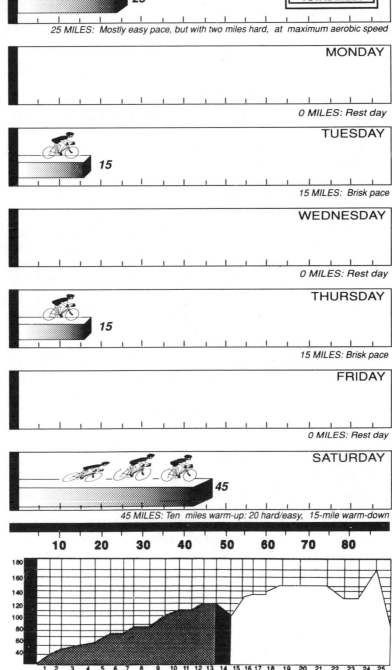

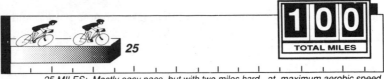

100 TOTAL MILES

25

25 MILES: Mostly easy pace, but with two miles hard, at maximum aerobic speed

WEEK 14

Miles are reduced to allow high-effort riding. In each 4-mile hard/easy set 2 miles are at maximum aerobic capacity, and 2 miles are at a twiddle. This builds aerobic capacity and climbing ability.

MONDAY

0 MILES: Rest day

TUESDAY

15

15 MILES: Brisk pace

WEDNESDAY

0 MILES: Rest day

THURSDAY

15

15 MILES: Brisk pace

FRIDAY

0 MILES: Rest day

SATURDAY

45

45 MILES: Ten miles warm-up: 20 hard/easy, 15-mile warm-down

TOTAL
FITNESS BASE
MILES
1268

hour. If you do have more time than that, take advantage of it and put a longer, harder ride in mid-week. Two long rides per week are enough. Remember, there is some glycogen depletion involved here, and you need time to recover from it.

Weeks 17 and 18—total, 150 miles

Sunday, 30 miles, easy twiddle

Monday, 15 miles, brisk pace

Wednesday, 15 miles, brisk pace

Friday, 15 miles, brisk pace

Saturday, 75 miles. Ten-mile warm-up, 55 miles brisk, ten-mile warm-down. All we added to the schedule so far was another midday ride. Now we'll add a few miles to the weekends.

Weeks 19, 20, 21—total, 160 miles

Sunday, 35 miles, easy twiddle

Monday, 15 miles, brisk pace

Wednesday, 15 miles, brisk pace

Friday, 15 miles, brisk pace

Saturday, 80 miles. Ten-mile warm-up, 60 miles brisk, ten-mile warm-down.

These mileages are high enough so that you really need to watch for overtraining symptoms. Given time, almost anyone can ride this much mileage and more, and many riders will find it easy to conquer the gradual increase from week to week. But even the best of us find that sometimes we have to abandon neat-looking goals drawn up on paper. The body demands a rest. If this happens, be realistic and cut back drastically to half the scheduled mileage for a week or two.

One way to avert overtraining symptoms is to make a mileage cutback deliberately. That is a good excuse to throw in more speedwork. You'll see that I have even cut back the Sunday ride, to give you more pent-up energy for the week's big ride:

GEARS ON TOUR

Will you be touring with panniers? Everyone says you should put the panniers on for all your training rides.

You weren't born to be a pack mule, and probably won't follow that advice.

If so, be prepared for a surprise on departure day: you'll be using much, much lower gears than you're used to.

When I'm fit enough to spin an 85-inch gear on flat ground without a load, I'll want about a 60-inch gear after adding panniers, a sleeping bag, and tent. Why such a drastic drop? The added weight doesn't increase rolling resistance that much. But it adds greatly to any teeny uphill you encounter, it demands more power during the dead spots

in your pedal stroke, and it makes it more difficult for you to accelerate. All these factors add up to make a lower cruising gear more comfortable and practical. And 90 rpm in a 60-inch gear gives 16 mph—a comfortably brisk touring speed.

On uphills, the loaded bike knows no substitute for bulldog gears. The inner chain ring yields a 1:1 27-inch gear on my touring bike, and a 25-inch gear on our touring tandem. I used to believe such gears were for sissies but now know better, and enjoy riding more because of it.

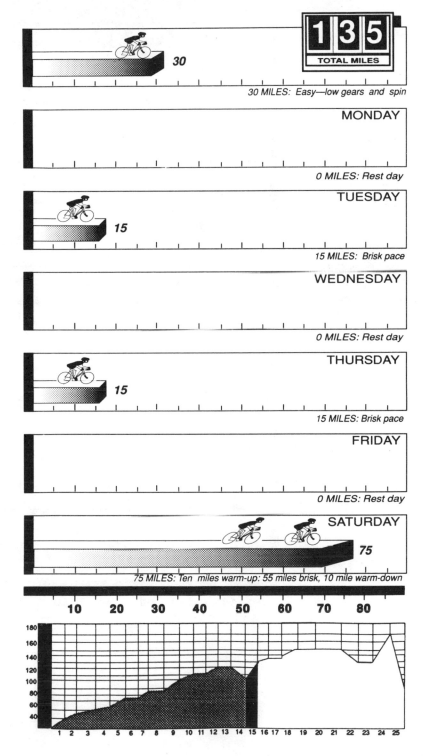

30 MILES: Easy—low gears and spin

135 TOTAL MILES

WEEK 15

This week jumps to 135 miles, but effort levels are cut back.
You should be feeling fairly comfortable with Saturday's 75-mile ride.

MONDAY

30

0 MILES: Rest day

TUESDAY

15

15 MILES: Brisk pace

WEDNESDAY

0 MILES: Rest day

THURSDAY

15

15 MILES: Brisk pace

FRIDAY

0 MILES: Rest day

SATURDAY

75

75 MILES: Ten miles warm-up: 55 miles brisk, 10 mile warm-down

TOTAL FITNESS BASE MILES
1403

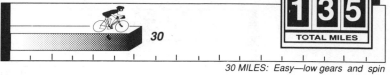

30

135 TOTAL MILES

30 MILES: Easy—low gears and spin

WEEK 16
Saturday's second 75-mile work-out will set you up to complete a 100-mile century without strain. You've reached a very definite level of fitness

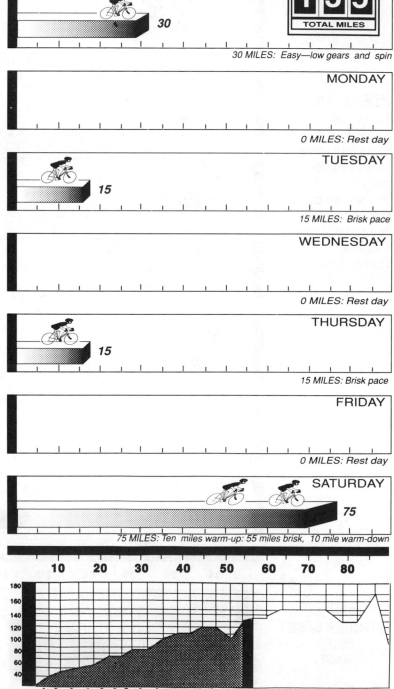

MONDAY

0 MILES: Rest day

TUESDAY

15

15 MILES: Brisk pace

WEDNESDAY

0 MILES: Rest day

THURSDAY

15

15 MILES: Brisk pace

FRIDAY

0 MILES: Rest day

SATURDAY

75

75 MILES: Ten miles warm-up: 55 miles brisk, 10 mile warm-down

10   20   30   40   50   60   70   80

TOTAL FITNESS BASE MILES **1538**

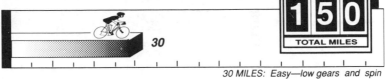

30 MILES: Easy—low gears and spin

TOTAL MILES 1 5 0

MONDAY

15

15 MILES: Brisk pace

WEEK 17

Week 17 calls for
five rides a week.
It may take you a
few days to
become used
to the change

TUESDAY

0 MILES: Rest day

WEDNESDAY

15

15 MILES: Brisk pace

THURSDAY

0 MILES: Rest day

FRIDAY

15

15 MILES: Brisk pace

SATURDAY

75

75 MILES: Ten miles warm-up: 55 miles brisk, 10 mile warm-down

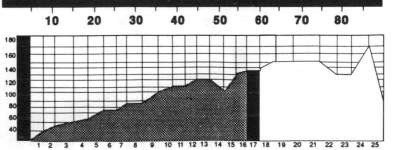

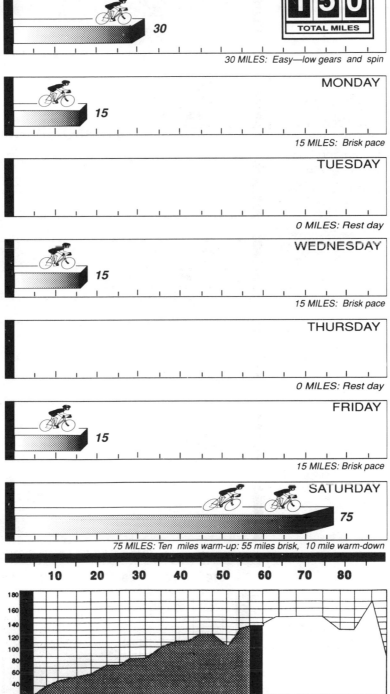

TOTAL
FITNESS BASE
MILES
1688

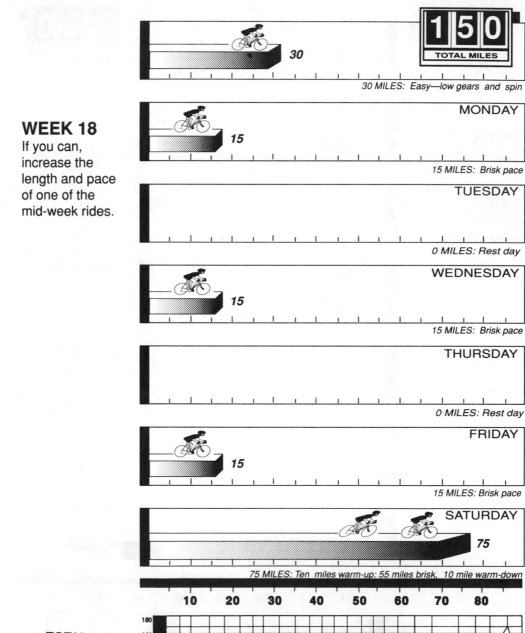

150
TOTAL MILES

30

30 MILES: Easy—low gears and spin

WEEK 18
If you can,
increase the
length and pace
of one of the
mid-week rides.

MONDAY

15

15 MILES: Brisk pace

TUESDAY

0 MILES: Rest day

WEDNESDAY

15

15 MILES: Brisk pace

THURSDAY

0 MILES: Rest day

FRIDAY

15

15 MILES: Brisk pace

SATURDAY

75

75 MILES: Ten miles warm-up: 55 miles brisk, 10 mile warm-down

10   20   30   40   50   60   70   80

TOTAL
FITNESS BASE
MILES
1838

WEEK 19

The miles are increasing steadily. Watch for overtraining and cut back on the miles if necessary.

WEEK 20

Same as week 19. Most people can handle this schedule, but do not press too hard. If your body says no, cut down the mileage.

WEEK 21

Same as week 20. If you are comfortable now, then you have the fitness base for the final weeks of training.

TOTAL FITNESS BASE MILES **2318**

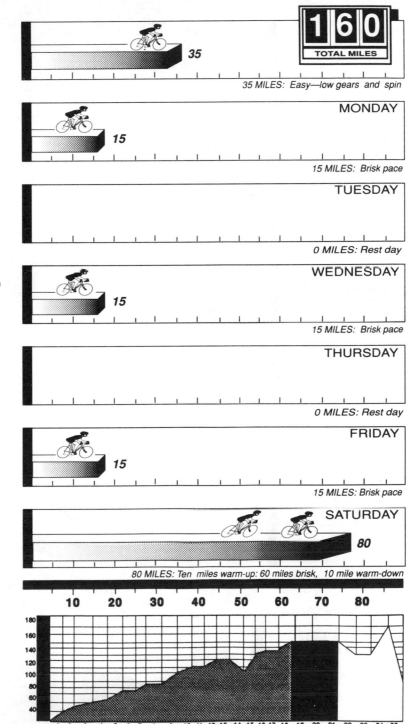

1 6 0 TOTAL MILES

35

35 MILES: Easy—low gears and spin

MONDAY

15

15 MILES: Brisk pace

TUESDAY

0 MILES: Rest day

WEDNESDAY

15

15 MILES: Brisk pace

THURSDAY

0 MILES: Rest day

FRIDAY

15

15 MILES: Brisk pace

SATURDAY

80

80 MILES: Ten miles warm-up: 60 miles brisk, 10 mile warm-down

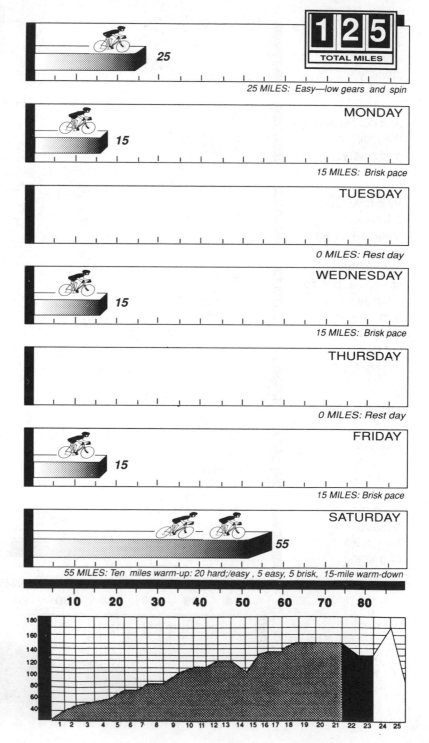

1 2 5
TOTAL MILES

25 MILES: Easy—low gears and spin

MONDAY

15 MILES: Brisk pace

TUESDAY

0 MILES: Rest day

WEDNESDAY

15 MILES: Brisk pace

THURSDAY

0 MILES: Rest day

FRIDAY

15 MILES: Brisk pace

SATURDAY

55 MILES: Ten miles warm-up: 20 hard;/easy , 5 easy, 5 brisk, 15-mile warm-down

WEEK 22
The distances are reduced but there are 20 miles of speedwork on Saturday's ride.

WEEK 23
This is the last week with speedwork. Give it the business.

TOTAL FITNESS BASE MILES 2568

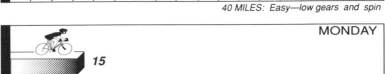

40 MILES: Easy—low gears and spin

170
TOTAL MILES

WEEK 24

Week 24 is slow and easy, to build up energy. Resist the temptation to show how strong you are and let your body build up reserves.

MONDAY

15 MILES: Brisk pace

TUESDAY

0 MILES: Rest day

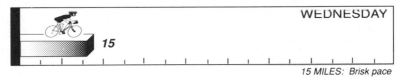

WEDNESDAY

15 MILES: Brisk pace

THURSDAY

0 MILES: Rest day

FRIDAY

15 MILES: Brisk pace

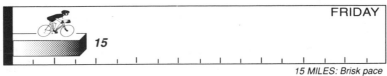

SATURDAY

85

85 MILES: Ten miles warm-up: 60 milles brisk, 10-mile warm-down

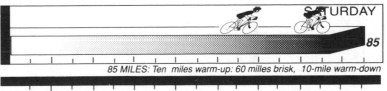

TOTAL FITNESS BASE MILES **2738**

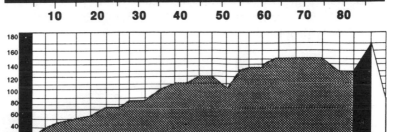

Weeks 22 and 23—total, 125 miles
 Sunday, 25 miles, easy twiddle
 Monday, 15 miles, brisk pace
 Wednesday, 15 miles, brisk pace
 Friday, 15, miles, brisk pace Saturday, 55 miles. Ten-mile warm-up, 20 miles divided into five sets of four miles per set. Each set contains two miles at maximum aerobic speed, two recovering at easy twiddle. Five miles easy twiddle. Five miles at brisk pace, ten-mile warm-down

Now it's time to peak for the next century. To do that, I recommend an LSD week—your longest yet—and a slow, easy week, to give you pent-up energy for the century.

Week 24—total, 170 miles
 Sunday, 40 miles, easy twiddle
 Monday, 15 miles, brisk pace
 Wednesday, 15 miles, brisk pace
 Friday, 15 miles, brisk pace
 Saturday, 85 miles. Ten-mile warm-up, 60 miles brisk, ten-mile warm-down.

Week 25—total, 95 miles
 Sunday, 25 miles, easy twiddle
 Monday, 15 miles, brisk pace
 Wednesday, 15 miles, brisk pace
 Friday, 15 miles, brisk pace
 Saturday, 25 miles, easy twiddle

And now you're ready to eat 100 miles for breakfast! Remember the warm-up, warm-down, leg massage, food and drink. You'll feel incredibly fit and ready for the ride. After the ride, have a nice hot bath and another leg massage, and you'll feel refreshed the following day.

Six months ago, the mere thought of 100 miles was an ordeal. Now it's just something you do.

Many riders will find this intensity level about all they care to engage in. You've cracked the big nut—a century—and by developing the pedalling technique and bike handling skills I've outlined, you may ride a pretty fast century on this reasonable level of training.

But what if you want to go faster?

There's a saying among coaches: 'You have to harden steel before you can temper it'. These work-outs have hardened you. If you want 'tempering'—a higher aerobic cruise speed, more aggressive climbing speed, etc—you now have the training base to go for it. Gains will come with greater difficulty now. But there's no thrill like speed, and speed is a reward many people crave.

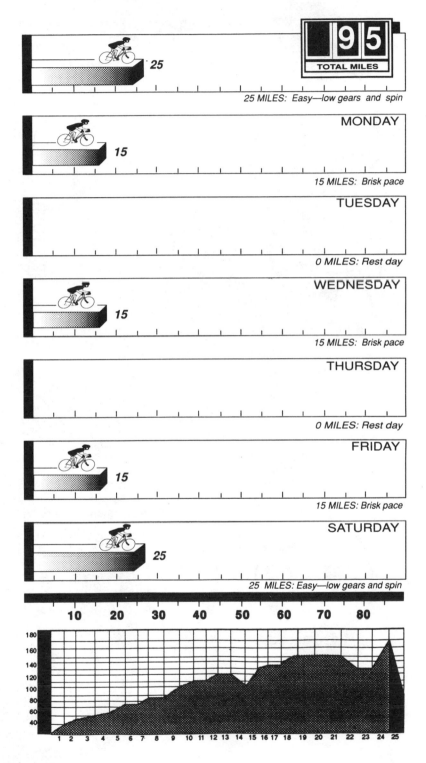

95 TOTAL MILES

25 MILES: Easy—low gears and spin

MONDAY

15 MILES: Brisk pace

TUESDAY

0 MILES: Rest day

WEDNESDAY

15 MILES: Brisk pace

THURSDAY

0 MILES: Rest day

FRIDAY

15 MILES: Brisk pace

SATURDAY

25 MILES: Easy—low gears and spin

WEEK 25

Week 25 is
a modest
95 miles. It's to
set you up so
you can eat
100 miles for
breakfast in
style!

TOTAL
FITNESS BASE
MILES
2833

Training
to Race

Contents

You will never, never feel more alive than when you're in a bike race. It's like flying in a swarm of bees. Riding that close to so many other riders going so fast is an over whelmingly intense experience. The peloton works together, utilizing the drafting effect to go faster than you would have ever dared try on your own. You stand and hammer huge gears to stay with the pack as it sprints up short hills; you gasp for air as the mountain goats among you set the pace on long hills, trying to drop the flatlanders.

On flats, the time trial specialists set the pace so you can sit in and spin your 52/13/108-inch gear; on descents, that gear is spun out and you need the utmost technique to stay with the pack. Those who let their attention drift, even for a second, are unceremoniously spit out the back. You work hard and stay alert. Occasionally you even go to the front and take a pull.

Talk about fun!

No other athletic event requires the same combination of tactics, alertness, aerobic horsepower, and sprinting ability to say nothing of bike handling. It's exacting and demanding—but if you're well prepared, even your first race can be exciting and rewarding.

That's a big 'if.' Most budding bike racers are baptised by failure, typically in a criterium (circuit race held on closed city streets). Let me describe a classic denouement, not to be negative, but to give you some idea of what to avoid:

The pack takes off at the gun at blinding sprint speed. You're caught at the back behind some slow riders. You try to get around them, but the leaders are already 100 yards ahead. The pack rounds the first corner, and the congestion delays you more while the leaders keep on going. You spend the next few laps sprinting as best you can, trying to catch up, but the lead pack pulls out of sight. By now, you're tiring from all that frantic effort, and slowing down.

The pace car comes up behind. You're lapped. An official tells you to get off the course. And that's it—for you, the race is over. To add insult to injury, you watch the lead riders slack off to a pace you could easily have maintained. They've done their dirty work and dropped half the field. Now they conserve their energy so they can outsprint each other at the finish. Systematic training will help you to avoid such problems.

Time Trials

To start your racing career off right, begin with time trials. When you've ridden a half-dozen club time trials, you're better prepared to judge when to try a criterium. If you prefer road races to criteriums and there are some where you live, great! However, although road races are the kind of event many riders prefer, they can be hard to locate.

Time trials aren't as exciting as mass-start races. The riders are sent off at one-minute intervals, so most of the time you can barely see another rider on the course. It's just you, alone with your throbbing heart. If you pass another rider, or are passed, you don't draft. Generally, you can't even add excitement with a sprint at the end—by then, you're too tired.

But time trials are safer for novices, give you a good gauge of your fitness and progress, and provide an introduction to fast riding at full effort. The stopwatch tells you how your efforts compare with those of seasoned racers—and whether you might be able to hold their wheel in a criterium. Any rider can enter an informal club time trial. Most

MAKE YOUR OWN OLYMPICS

Sometimes the club time trial is out of town. Sometimes it's out of season. For whatever reason, you need a time trial course you can ride yourself, any time you feel the urge. You can devise your own course easily and make it the scene of your own private Olympics, as you break the half-hour barrier. Discarded bottle caps from a parking lot can be your Olympic medals!

Here are the course requirements:
● A bare minimum of seven miles; a maximum of 12.
● As flat as possible. This assumes that the course is to gauge your fitness for time trialling and criteriums. If you'll be riding hilly road races, you'll want another time trial course with some hills, but also with a flat start/finish area.
● Start/finish area at least five miles from your house, to enforce an honest warm-up and warm-down.
● Lightly travelled roads in good condition.

In conventional time trials, you get a standing start; someone holds your bike upright by the saddle, so you can be ready with both feet in the toe clips. For your self-timed effort, a rolling start will be far more practical.

If you want to calibrate your course's length, don't use a car odometer—they can easily be five per cent inaccurate. You'll get much more accurate results by tracing the course on Ordnance Survey maps, which are drawn to an extremely accurate standard. With OS 1:50,000 scale maps, you can easily calibrate the course length to 200 feet, perhaps even to 100 feet. These maps are also far and away the easiest way to find a good course in the first place. One thing you'll soon discover is that a course with corners in it slows you down more than you'd ever guess. My local racing club uses a 2.37-mile loop with four corners. Yet, even when we were under the delusion that the course was 2.5 miles, our four-lap times seemed a bit slower than we would have expected from the same riders' performances on certified 25-mile out-and-back courses. And this course was flat by our standards, too—only 50 feet of climbing and descending per lap.

clubs are happy to see a new face. Racing clubs hold weekly time trials during the racing season, or even year-round. Locate such a club by asking at area bike shops.

Most club time trials are around ten miles—long enough to tell you how your aerobic fitness is coming, but not so severe as to require days of recovery. The standard national championship time trial distance is 25 miles—a bit too long and gruelling for a weekly gauge of your fitness. If you ride a time trial correctly, you'll feel pretty wiped out for the next few days.

If you've been doing some of the work-outs in the past chapter, and think you have a brisk maximum aerobic speed, by all means, go ahead and enter a time trial. Don't forget to warm up! You can't once the ride has started.

There's little ceremony: the man says 'go', and that's what you do. The incentive of the stopwatch makes this no ordinary ride, though. You sprint up to your cruising speed as abruptly as possible. You're breathing hard right from the gun. A small lactic acid singe in your quads punishes you for that starting gun sprint. But this time, you don't get to relax and let the lactic acid go away—that would slow you down a few costly seconds.

You immediately upshift to your cruise gear and begin pounding it, determinedly hanging onto your momentum. At this high speed, only the most crouched, aerodynamic body position is workable. Even if you sit up for a second, just long enough to take a sip from your water bottle, you feel tremendous aerodynamic drag.

Every tiny uphill demands extra effort. You try to maintain your velocity by hammering over hills without slowing or downshifting. You stand, sacrificing aerodynamics for a temporary infusion of power. But what a standing position! You keep your head low and arms bent, all for aerodynamics. When you've crested a hill, you hope you can ease off effort and still maintain your speed, so you can recover your breath on the downslope.

(This makes sense according to the laws of physics. Additional effort garners you more speed/time on an uphill than on a downhill. On an uphill, the effort of lifting your weight becomes an important component of your overall effort, and that effort increases directly with your groundspeed. On the downhill, though, there's no lifting involved, and virtually all your effort is used to overcome wind resistance. That effort increases with the cube of the airspeed.)

On longer hills, you stay seated and reluctantly gear down. No sense blowing up. You should always feel a slight lactic acid burn and be breathing quickly. This isn't a comfortable event for the not-quite-in-shape rider.

If there are corners, get through them quickly, using a sharp lean angle to maintain your speed. If there's a turnaround, maintain your speed until just before the turnaround, brake abruptly, turn quickly, and sprint back up to cruising speed.

Maintain a high effort level so that when you near the finish, you won't feel like sprinting. Try to sprint anyway. Reach for those last few seconds. Then stay on the bike and warm down with some light twiddling.

Most time triallists find they ride faster if they grind a slightly bigger gear than they feel entirely comfortable with. At the national champion level, riders mix 55-tooth chainrings with 12-tooth cogs! But please, start your time trialling career without anything so drastic. You may want to invest in a straight-block freewheel for flat time trials. Straight blocks are horrid devices, useless for any fun riding outside of flat Fenlands. But they allow you to select the exact gear you need in the heat of competition.

Straight blocks usually come with teeth of 13-14-15-16-17-18. Few amateur riders can really spin a 52/13 without drafting another rider or descending hills steeper than those found on most time trial courses. I prefer to have a 14-19 straight block for time trialling. The 19-tooth is useful for accelerating from the start or out of corners, or for climbing the semi-gentle hills that sneak into many time trial courses. Since I'm no pro rider, I do most of my riding in 52/16 at a cadence unusually brisk by time trial standards. You may prefer 52/15 or 52/14 but probably not in your first competitive time trial. Sample the event before you rush out and buy more equipment.

Interval Training

Riding faster and hurting less requires more intense training. The training base in the last chapter will give the easy gains in aerobic speed. Now you want the hard gains, and they come from interval training.

If you've opened the book at this page, go back to the section on early-season miles. A bare minimum of 1,000 miles is necessary before you begin interval training. Riders who religiously log 150 miles per week in the off season (as opposed to those of us who try to make up for lost time each April) start their intervals after a base of 1,500 or 2,000 miles.

There's nothing mysterious about how to do intervals. You put out a high level of effort for a set time, distance, number of pedal strokes, or until the third telephone pole. Ease back to a twiddle until you feel ready to repeat the hard effort. Then do it again.

Done properly, intervals hurt. They bring your pulse, breathing, and all other body functions to top speed and keep them there for a long time. It's common to feel slight nausea, a weak feeling in the chest, and an overall limpness, which you somehow set aside to attack the next interval.

I know I told you cycling didn't have to hurt, but I wasn't talking then about training to do well in time trials.

Intervals are essential because the body conditions itself only for the exercise you give it. You have to train your body for your performance goal indirectly. If you want to ride, say, 25 mph for one hour, you have to get your body used to sustained output for longer than one hour (that's your LSD training, well below 25 mph). Plus, you have to ride above 25 mph for two or three minutes in order for some training effect to set in.

If you can, do interval work-outs with other riders who share the same goals. It's fantastic if you can go with riders a bit faster than you; trying to stay up with them helps you go faster than you could riding alone, contemplating the silos on the horizon. When I ride intervals with others, we don't draft during the hard part unless a rider clearly needs help to avoid getting dropped. We use phone poles or other landmarks for our start and finish lines—easier than synchronizing watches.

It's Wednesday afternoon and you want to ride faster in next Saturday's time trial. Let's do some intervals. After the now-familiar Long and Beneficial Warm up, you find a quiet stretch of road. Whether you go by time, distance or pedal strokes is really up to you, but for simplicity's sake I'll use time. With a stopwatch strapped to your handlebars where you can see it, accelerate to a tough, slightly-higher-than-aerobic speed that you can maintain for two minutes. Then do so. Hold that speed! A speedometer helps, but don't let the lack of one be an excuse. You can feel it in your bones if you start to slack off.

At the end of two minutes, back off to an easy twiddle and relax until you're somewhat recovered. In the old days, we waited until our breathing had slowed down and we were almost able to talk easily. Today's more avant garde scientific method is to wait until your pulse drops to 120. (The more fit you are, the more quickly your body will recover and your pulse will drop.) Either way, you're apt to feel weak and empty, even though the guidelines say you're recovered. Don't be fooled. Deep down you have the necessary suds to do another high-quality two-minute interval.

So do it again.

And again.

Three of these are more than enough for your first stab at intervals. A fourth would likely be a failure—you'd be unable to keep up speed, and you'd hurt more.

Theoretically, you can fit intervals into a short work-out. Twelve miles of interval madness, a five-mile warm-up and three-mile warm-down only 20 miles. But if you possibly can, sandwich intervals into the middle of a longer ride, so both your warm-up, and warm-down are longer. Runners and swimmers may gripe at the vague, hand-waving terminology I have used to tell you how fast to go. Your coaches always told you how many laps, how many minutes and seconds per lap, and how many seconds of recovery between efforts. But there's no universal measure that translates to your individual fitness, or to the streets you ride on. Some coaches use terms such as '75 per cent' effort. That kind of description *sounds* precise, but asks you to measure a feeling numerically! I prefer to describe effort levels in relation to your anaerobic threshold, which you should know by now.

Just as the secret police use both the thumbscrew and the rack to give their captive audience some variety, there are several kinds of intervals you can enjoy. You can change the distance of the hard effort, mix different distances on a single day, tamper with your recovery time, or mix big-gear intervals with little-gear intervals. There are lots of ways to have fun, and every one of them has an important purpose, a nuance of specific training.

Three- to five-minute intervals will help gain the conditioning needed for longer time trials. It's a rare rider that can do these well alone. It's just too human to slack off sometime during the four long minutes of accumulating lactic acid and a pounding heart. If you can find a willing riding companion, even a passive one who will sit on your wheel and blandly mumble 'nice pull you took there', bring him along.

Often, your training needs will dictate short intervals to improve your sprint. A typical sprint interval work-out would be five rides of one minute at all-you-can-stand effort, or five all-out sprints spanning the 200 yards between two adjacent telephone poles. The distance ridden may appear modest—five sets of something less than half a mile per set doesn't seem a lot but you'll quickly find that you simply can't ride more than that and keep the intensity level high. These are demanding efforts. And all-out sprints use 40 times more glucose than steady-state riding, so by the third sprint you might not have as much glucose available as the muscles are asking for.

Riders who were born for long distances will find they simply can't ride short interval work-outs in the early season. If you are one of these, have patience. After 1,500 miles and some longer, slower interval work-outs, that snap in your legs will come alive and you'll be able to really put yourself into short sprint work-outs. You may even surprise yourself by the company you keep up with; good mid-season training has sometimes allowed me to ride credible work-outs with track sprinters far superior to me on the track.

Mixing distances on a single day is a way to add important psychological variety and a mix of training benefits. Ride three-minute, two-minute, and one-minute hard efforts with plenty of recovery in between. Then, after an especially ample recovery, repeat the two-minute and one-minute rides and limp home. You'll be a faster rider for it after a few days' rest, honest!

Another slant on interval training is the interval without a reasonable rest period. This is a good one—it simulates race conditions! It teaches you how deep you can dig for those last hard pedal strokes, and also how much you can make out of a brief semi-resting period. These, too, are best done with other like-minded riders.

Initially, I recommend that the hard work segments be regular and predictable—five phone poles hard, four phone poles easy, repeat, that sort of thing. Otherwise, your bleary-eyed group of riders will get confused.

After your group has mastered basic timing—and the co-ordination is far from simple—you can designate a leader to start and stop the mayhem with shouted commands; he can vary the distances and spring surprises on you. That, too, simulates race conditions.

Big gear/little gear intervals may be the most humane twist on this whole business, because they allow refreshing variety. Ride the first and third intervals on the big chain ring, the second and fourth on the little chainring. The change is good for you; many top racers have used and recommended this trick.

Interval work-outs can make overtraining come that much easier. You should start out with just one in your weekly schedule. Then after a month of that, maybe you can add a second hard work-out. If you insist on going to three tough work-outs per week, mix speed work-outs with long distance work-outs. And when your basal pulse rises each morning, and that listless feeling tells you you're overtraining, back off.

Here's how you might put one of these work-outs into a weekly schedule (note: by now I'm assuming you can find training time on weekdays.):

Sunday, 30 miles easy twiddle

Monday, 25 miles. Five miles warm-up, 15 miles brisk to stiff, five miles warm-down

Tuesday, 15 miles easy twiddle

Wednesday, 40 miles. Intervals. Fifteen miles warm-up, three sets of two minutes on/two minutes off, totalling about four miles. Six miles easy twiddle to recover. Ten miles brisk, five miles warm-down.

Thursday, 15 miles, easy twiddle

Saturday, 55 miles. Five miles warm-up and warm-down, 45 miles brisk. Or ride your club time trial, and enough mileage afterwards to add up to a good daily mileage. Total, 195 miles.

This is a typical good training week for a non-professional bike racer. You could still work for a living in the remaining time, and be fit enough to enjoy your racing.

Racing Tactics

When your training reaches a level with several styles of interval work-out, including some sprint work-outs, you're almost ready to attack your first criterium in style and stay with the field until the finish. Your final preparation for that criterium will be some mighty frisky group rides. There are some new group riding exercises for this: leadouts, blocking, breaking away, and bridging gaps. These exercises are the ABCs of team tactics. To practise most of them effectively, you need a minimum of four riders.

It always helps to go watch some races and see these tactics in action. Sometimes you'll see a negative, defensive race, with everyone trying to sit in and avoid working. But you'll also see breakaways and blocking succeed, and that's inspiring.

Why practise team tactics, when most women's and entry-level men's criteriums are too disorganized to have any? Two reasons:

One, practicing a few elementary tactics is as good a way as any to teach you to respond to the peleton's unpredictable whims.

Two, if you and your cohorts work as a team, you can control the race. After the mad dash of the first few laps dies down, you wait for the right moment. When no one else is looking, you send two or three riders off the front and deploy the rest of the riders to sit at the front of the field, slowing the pace and sabotaging everyone else's efforts to chase. Or, if a breakaway isn't possible, you lead your best sprinter into position just before the finish, so he wins easily.

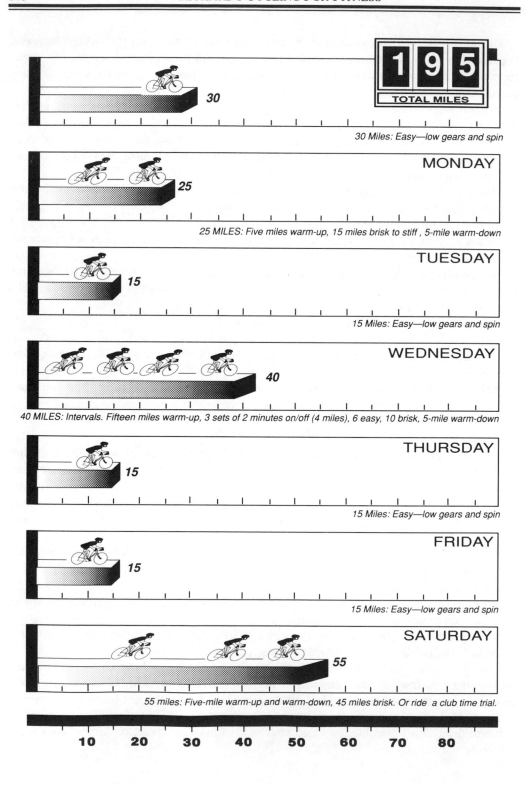

195

TOTAL MILES

30

30 Miles: Easy—low gears and spin

MONDAY

25

25 MILES: Five miles warm-up, 15 miles brisk to stiff , 5-mile warm-down

TUESDAY

15

15 Miles: Easy—low gears and spin

WEDNESDAY

40

40 MILES: Intervals. Fifteen miles warm-up, 3 sets of 2 minutes on/off (4 miles), 6 easy, 10 brisk, 5-mile warm-down

THURSDAY

15

15 Miles: Easy—low gears and spin

FRIDAY

15

15 Miles: Easy—low gears and spin

SATURDAY

55

55 miles: Five-mile warm-up and warm-down, 45 miles brisk. Or ride a club time trial.

10   20   30   40   50   60   70   80

These tactics are easier said than done. Most beginning racers only read about them. But practise them and you may well pull them off.

Only a very large training group can even begin to simulate the mayhem of the pack, but only two people are needed to practise the co-ordination of a leadout, and learn the speeds, timing, and distance required.

The Leadout

A leadout is helping another rider do well in the final sprint. He sits on your wheel as you accelerate and move to the front of the pack. You keep your acceleration as smooth and

Attacker sits on wheel of leader and saves energy

Leader thrusts into opening in pack

even as it can be in the midst of all those other riders, to make it easy for your designated sprinter to stay on your wheel. If the pack is congested, you open holes that both of you can slip through. About 200 yards before the finish, you reach the front and swing off so he can sprint by.

In theory, he's all set to win the race. He's fully rested from drafting you, he's already going faster than the peleton's speed, and he's at the front. Some brisk pedal strokes on his part, and he's in the clear.

In practice, many things can go wrong. You may tire out and slow down before reach-

Leader moves to front of pack

ing the front. If you do what is human—try to struggle on valiantly, going slower all the while—the sprinter is stuck behind you, and has to expend effort to get around you. The two of you may get stuck behind someone else's block, whether intentional or not.

When you begin the leadout in practice sessions, accelerate slowly—usually without standing—and wind up to your top speed. (Because you've been fighting the air mass for the ten seconds necessary to wind up, you'll already feel a bit of sprint fatigue and your top speed won't be your absolute best.)

Look behind for overtaking traffic and swing off—or, by prearrangement, sit tight when your partner comes around you. If his sprint is any good, he should be able to get around you in just a few pedal strokes; by the time his rear tyre is clear of your front tyre, he should be going much faster than you. There are several embellishments on leadouts. You can do them when you're fresh and again when you're tired, to see the effect of fatigue on your ability to co-ordinate the motions. When you've led your friend out, try to jump on his wheel. If he's got a good sprint, you won't have a chance. In a large group, leadouts can turn into a game of tag—send a rider ahead and lead out other riders to catch him.

About 200 yards from finish line, leader swings off and attacker sprints for a win

Make riders swing round you

The Block

Blocking is one of those nasty skills you need to use when a teammate goes off the front of the pack. You have to be ready to move to the front. When you get there, slack off. Make the other riders come around you to pick the pace up—when they do, get on their wheels and into position to move to the front again. Spend as much time in front as possible. If you're in the middle of a smooth paceline formed by the other riders, make sure it doesn't stay smooth. Let gaps open, and make other riders do the work to close them.

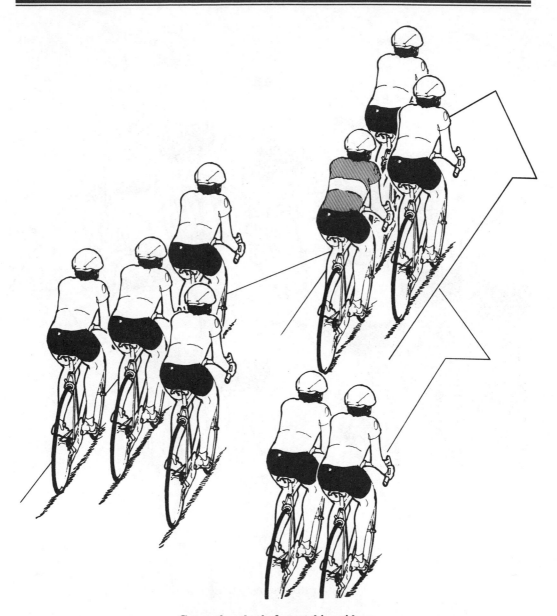

Get on the wheel of overtaking riders

What if you have to go much faster than the field? You may need to bridge a gap from one group of riders to another, or establish a breakaway and get it comfortably out of sight of the field, or lead your sprinter up through the field. You may need to chase the field after a crash, a wheel change, or other mishap.

One-minute and two-minute duration intervals will help with this. Make these intervals into group riding games. Sit up, relax briefly, and send your strongest rider ahead by himself. When he gets 200 yards away, chase him down with a designated sprinter on your wheel. Then the three of you sprint for the crest of the hill or the next phone pole. Two hundred yards may seem like an inhumanely long gap to bridge, but bike races often demand more than that from you. All these tactics *sound* easy, but wait until you try them in race conditions. It's hard enough to get them right in practice. For one thing, you'll find it tough to be where you want to be in the pack. You may not have the suds to stay near the front constantly. If your goal is to stay, say, one third back, you'll find the pack constantly moving around. You can't just sit on one guy's wheel and hold your position; he'll speed up and slow down, and riders will be constantly milling around.

No matter how eager you are to sit on a wheel and rest, you have to be ready to sprint all out at any moment. It's just tough if you're tired, or if you want to rest because you just took a pull. Sometimes the pack just picks up and goes, and you have to react instantly and go with it. You may get a chance to sit in and rest later, but you don't get to pick the time. If you try to conserve any effort when the pack is jamming, you're out of the race.

You may want to race before you've gone through all the training exercises I've outlined here. No law against it—they'll happily take your entry fee. But you won't like the results.

I learned the hard way about the need to train for a variety of tasks. During one season I did a perfect set of work-outs to peak for a 25-mile time trial, finishing the event in one hour, one minute, and a bunch of seconds for my best racing performance ever.

Five days later, I rode a 4,000-metre pursuit on the track, in a ridiculously slow time. The pursuit wasn't even ten per cent of the length of the time trial, but I rode both races at virtually the same speed! I had a top speed, and that was it. Anything faster I could only manage for ten pedal strokes at a time—not

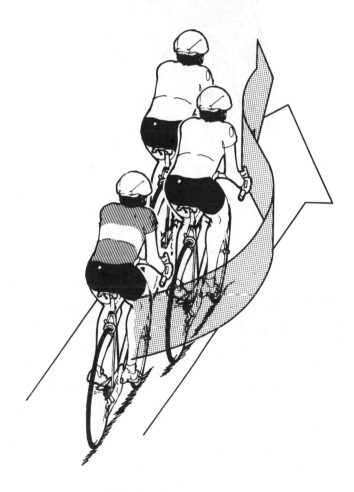

Use speed advantage of drafting to pass

And then slow down again

much of a sprint. Needless to say, I got dropped right away in the one criterium I entered that season.

Group exercises can be plugged into your schedule much like the speed work-out in the time trialist's schedule. Stretch your bike handling skills. In a race you'll have to corner more quickly than ever, so do the best you can in training. Practise sprinting full speed into a sharp corner, waiting until the last possible moment before braking hard, leaning and turning sharply, and then sprinting out of the corner. Work with your training companions to hone these skills, simulating race conditions in training as much as is humanly possible.

Your time trial mates probably hold training mass-start races, or know someone who does. Try a few training races and then go for that criterium. You've done all the preparation you can.

Riding a Criterium

Make a checklist of equipment the night before. Don't forget a shoe, the spare shoelaces, or spare wheels if you have them. You want to be able to take your equipment for granted on race day. Don't use any equipment in a race that has less than 50 training miles; every new piece of equipment takes getting used to, and defective tyres sometimes take that long to show their dark side. Try like crazy to get a good position on the starting grid, but remember that your gap-bridging exercises will redeem you if you get stuck at the back.

Each race has its own personality; be ready for whatever it turns out to be. A race can be erratic, speeding up and slowing down for no apparent reason. It can be hard at first, and then slow down. I've become lulled into a sense of false security by races that troll at touring speed for miles, then break loose and go like hell. I might have expected that from a 100-mile road race, wherein everyone wants to warm up for a while, but these were short races, under 25 miles.

Bike races are ruthless Darwinian events, quickly separating survivors from those doomed to extinction. If they can, your competitors will use every one of your weaknesses to drop you.

Sprinting, climbing, and descending are obvious examples. Another is brisk cornering at the front, in a manner hard for others to follow, to string out the pack and leave off the slow cornerers.

How do you measure success in a bike race? Normally, the officials only count the first five places; it is somewhat deflating to come home and say, 'I finished'. And sometimes you can't even say that, because it's a brutal race full of ex-Olympic athletes and you don't even finish. But you can say, 'It took those hammerheads 25 miles to drop me', and be justly proud. This sounds bleak, particularly to anyone who's plodded through a 10K foot race in 55 minutes and received the T-shirt, ribbon, time, place, and polite applause.

But bike races are more exciting than 10Ks, and the 55-minute man never proved he could go ten feet at the winner's pace. Sometimes you enter a tough race and get lucky: a personal breakthrough in performance, all the right tactical moves, and lady luck brings you a storybook race—it does happen.

Road Racing

Time-trialling is widespread in Britain because mass-start road races were banned decades ago. Road racing has always been popular on the Continent, however, and is now reviving in Britain.

Road races have more of the romance of long-distance running and more complex strategy and team tactics than criteriums. Long hills favour the climbers, long descents favour the well-co-ordinated peloton. A road race may be 20 miles or 100. You can't get a very satisfying tactical game in 20 miles, and only the fittest riders can last for 100. Races from 40 to 60 miles are ideal for most beginning road racers.

The stereotype 100-mile-long road race has a slow start, as the riders make a silent pact to warm up easily. But don't count on it. Sometimes the longest race will sprint from the gun. The pace may be smooth and steady, or it may be erratic, with lots of braking and sprinting alternated for no apparent reason.

The work-outs given so far cover most of the abilities needed for road racing. Plan less sprinting and more long-duration intervals. The ability to ride much faster than the pack for two to five minutes, to catch or establish a break group, is an essential component of your road race strategy, and some lung-burning four-minute intervals will really help.

Two new abilities to emphasize in your work-outs are climbing and long distance. Long distance is somewhat self-evident. If a race lasts four hours and your training rides are only for two hours, you probably won't last the race. Some riders like 100- and 120-mile training rides; others find 80-mile training rides, which last as long as a 100-mile race, to be adequate.

Long distances mean a bigger time commitment to training. A 200-mile per week training schedule will get you in the field in road racing, but most good riders train more like 300 miles per week in season. A 300-mile week might look like this:

Sunday, 50 miles, mostly easy
Monday, 60 miles, motorpacing
Tuesday, 35 miles, mostly easy

TIME TRIAL EQUIPMENT

The urge to have the fanciest and most expensive equipment comes home to roost in time trials. At championship levels, everybody who's anybody uses a funny bike with disc wheels, upside down handlebars, and a quite uncomfortable riding position.

These bikes do make you go faster. Wind-tunnel tests confirm that a completely souped-up aerodynamic bike, with flat water bottle, airfoil handlebars, aero frame, and the works will be three minutes faster than a standard road racing bike over 25 miles. Of course, those three minutes aren't a reflection of the rider's fitness.

Don't buy a time trial bike for personal fitness. Spend the money instead on other equipment you'd use more often. Don't buy a time trial bike for daily training; the lack of an upright hand position will drive you crazy. But if you ride long time trials against riders on aero bikes, getting one for yourself will put you on an even footing.

What about less drastic equipment changes? Lighter wheels, a lighter frame, a skinsuit?

A lighter frame will not make a measurable difference in your time trial performance. It may feel better which is the reason, and the only reason, to buy one. Lighter wheels help, but not very much in a time trial. A medium-weight touring wheel with good tyres pumped up to full air pressure has only slightly higher rolling resistance than a light wheel. The advantage of light wheels is for pack racing; less energy is required for constant acceleration and deceleration. If you're lightweight and you don't ruin wheels often, 32-spoke wheels save considerable wind resistance. If you're a big guy, stick with the standard 36. A skinsuit saves measurable seconds.

But make your fitness the first goal, the equipment collection the second. If you crave a fancy new bike, reward yourself when you finally do break your 'personal best' for that club time trial.

Wednesday, 45 miles with hard intervals, sprints and climbs
Thursday, 20 miles, easy twiddle
Friday, 30 miles, easy twiddle; a couple of short sprints
Saturday, race 60 miles

It's the same thing as the other weeks you rode, only more of it. Monday, Wednesday and Saturday are the hard days. Since Saturday is race day, you get two rest days to recover for it. Of course, you need to work up to this schedule gradually. But when you do, you'll love it. Simply being fit enough to ride this much is a treat. The race results that follow are bonuses.

Practise eating and drinking on your training rides so you know what foods and beverages work for you and make your stomach feel good. Race day is no time to experiment.

Seemingly tiny procedural changes on race day can be major problems, as I learned in a 42-mile road race on an exceptionally hot July day. I deployed what I thought was a grand new formula for long-distance success. During a 65-mile training ride a week earlier, I'd felt an enormous boost when my partner and I stopped briefly and shared a can of Coke and drank some water. So I put dilute Coke, which I plucked from an ice chest minutes before the race started, in a water bottle.

Halfway through the race I reached for the Pause that Refreshes. The dilute Coke had warmed up to about 90 degrees; at that temperature, it tasted syrupy and uninviting. Then I couldn't get the water bottle back into the rack, which was an unconventional type. I hadn't had any problem with that rack before, but I'd never tried to use it at 25 mph amid

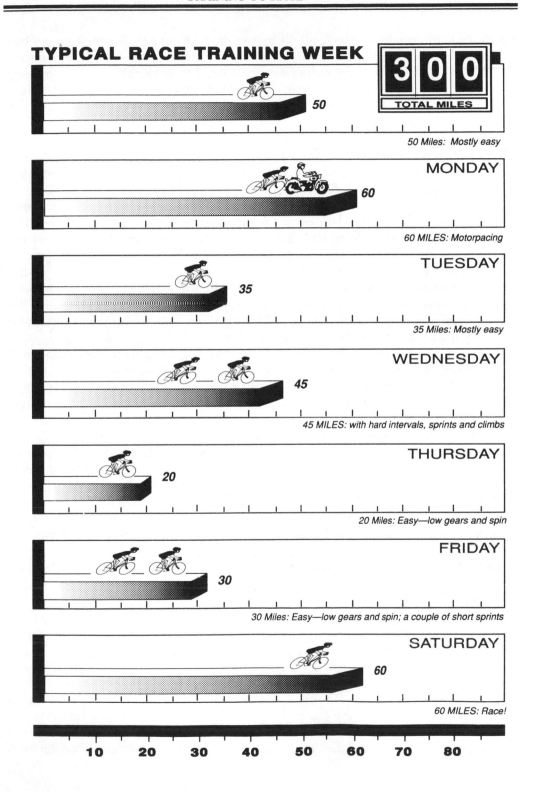

TYPICAL RACE TRAINING WEEK

300 TOTAL MILES

50

50 Miles: Mostly easy

MONDAY

60

60 MILES: Motorpacing

TUESDAY

35

35 Miles: Mostly easy

WEDNESDAY

45

45 MILES: with hard intervals, sprints and climbs

THURSDAY

20

20 Miles: Easy—low gears and spin

FRIDAY

30

30 Miles: Easy—low gears and spin; a couple of short sprints

SATURDAY

60

60 MILES: Race!

10 20 30 40 50 60 70 80

a pack. I had to slow down, dangle off the back of the pack, fuss about with the water bottle, and sprint to rejoin the pack. A pro would have donated the bottle to the nearest ditch!

The lesson is: everything you plan to do on race day, try out in training. If you're going to get food and water handed to you in the feed zone, practise that with your feeder. When race day comes, you'll be 60 miles tired and in the peleton—no time to learn new tricks.

Climbing

Great climbers are amazing. You worry that they'll suck all the oxygen out of the atmosphere. And when you have to maintain the pace they set in a race, you worry that they'll suck all the oxygen out of you.

Some riders have a psychological block against climbing; others love it. I've known riders who were great on the flats, but fell to pieces on relatively small climbs, and I've known others who were great climbers but not much else. The differences in performance are not explained just by differences in raw aerobic ability. Psychology plays a big part.

Some riders avoid the hills in training. For a track racer, concerned with his sprint, this is a good peaking strategy. (But some of his off-season miles should be in the hills for variety.) However, road riders need to get accustomed to how hills feel, and to learn to like the challenge of getting up a hill quickly. That means lots of work-outs in the hills, in the company of good climbers who are hard to stay with.

The true physiological differences between climbing and riding the flats are as follows:

The climber has to fight his own weight, so every pound less is a help.

When climbing, the bike wants to slow down more suddenly during the dead portions of the pedalling circle, between power strokes. This can make for more 'bobbing', energy-wasting speed surges with each pedal stroke.

And you have to choose between standing and seated climbing.

Standing climbing brings more of your body's muscles into play. Your back, arms, and shoulders get to share the work. They're used inefficiently, and you expend a lot of energy just holding them in position, but they do help propel the bike. By contrast, seated climbing puts all the work on your leg muscles. You can feel the difference by alternating between standing and seated climbing while maintaining a constant speed on a constant upgrade. You sense that the standing position is needlessly tiring out your upper body, yet it feels easier than staying seated, which makes your quads burn.

The other difference is that vigorous standing climbing is generally a glucose-burning activity—so you have to do it sparingly to last the race. As noted cycling author John Forester puts it: 'You have only so many good standing pedal strokes in you each day.'

So if you develop your quads to take the strain, seated climbing is more efficient. For that purpose, I recommend three- and four-minute intervals of painfully gruelling seated climbing up your favourite hill. Keep this a purely aerobic activity; sprint intervals would serve little purpose. Recover and do it again and again. Learn how big a gear you can comfortably maintain in training. No use getting halfway up the hill, in what turns out to be anaerobic effort, and then blowing up. When you do that in a race, the pack moves away from you so fast you think you're going backwards. In a race, spare no effort to stay with the pack. You may find yourself climbing hills in gears so tall they amaze you. That's to be expected. Poor climbers often try to get to the base of the hill at the front of the pack,

TRACK RACING WITHOUT TEARS

Track racing can be extremely exciting and fun. It's thought of as favouring the sprinter, but a 60-lap or 100-lap points race demands no small amount of overall conditioning.

Track racing is also a very specialized skill. It is close to suicide to buy a racing licence and a track bike, and then just show up and enter races without specialized training. Technically, you're allowed to do just that, but practically, you'll want the training. The few velodromes there are have development programmes for prospective racers of all ages.

Don't think you're too advanced for a basic bike riding class. Literally every manoeuvre you've learned on the road must be relearned on the track. The steep banking, no freewheel, and no brakes change everything. Holding a wheel without overshooting it, being able to overtake other riders and drop in front of them safely, and slipping into a small hole in the pack are three small examples of manoeuvres where brakes are usually used. Now, instead, you have to accelerate and deaccelerate using only the pedals, with precise force and timing.

New track riders generally get to race in short scratch races (simple five-lap races, for example), points races (longer races, probably 50 laps at first, with the winner determined on points won at intermediate sprints), and fun races such as the miss-and-out (in which the last rider across the line each lap is eliminated from the race.)

or ahead of the pack in a breakaway, so they'll still be in contact with the back of the pack at the top. If you do get dropped on the climb, put your nose down and chase right away.

Occasionally, you'll get lucky. The pack may take a breather at the summit, or a great flatland rider will have been dropped, too, so the two of you can chase together.

Well, what if you're one of the mountain goats? Deploy your ability craftily. It doesn't do you any good to be alone, 100 yards ahead of the guys at the top of every climb, and then sit up and wait for them to catch you. Perhaps you can use a long climb to initiate a solo break within a few miles of the finish. But if it's a short climb, don't kid yourself. (Those 50- and 100-foot elevation changes are called 'sprinters' hills', and guys who aren't really climbers somehow get up them faster than anyone else.) Or you can use your climbing ability to get away early in the race in a group with other riders.

Every manoeuvre you make in a bike race is a gamble. You go off the front and see if you can get a break group to form around you. Or you see a break forming and chase it down, not knowing if that's a strong enough group of people to stay away the rest of the afternoon. One rider might be a saboteur, working for a sprinter who's still back in the field. The possibilities are endless. Keep trying long shots, and one day you'll succeed.

Peaks and Valleys

Exercise tears the body down, and rest rebuilds it. This happens on many levels, both physical and psychological, and with many timetables. It takes two to four days to recover from a really hard work-out. But some things require a much longer recovery time, and you cannot doggedly ignore that in your training and racing.

Most of us cannot maintain a peak level of performance for more than a few weeks. Try to hold the peak longer and you will go stale. Better to back off, switch from speed work to easygoing LSD, and come back later for another peak, two to four months later.

Professionals are the living exception to this rule—they race literally every day from early spring to late autumn. And they try to perform consistently the entire time. But then, most of them go through their entire careers without winning races, even though they're very talented and fit athletes.

When your training and racing bring you to a peak, it feels great. Every day you feel stronger; you start dropping riders who used to drop you; your appetite for that fit feeling becomes insatiable, and you want to keep training more and more to feed that fire.

It doesn't last. Frustration awaits the rider who tries to keep the peak going longer than fate will allow. He'll just keep working out and keep going slower.

Pick the races you want to do really well in. From your base of several months' LSD training, concoct a ten-week training schedule to sharpen yourself with the right mix of speedwork, hills, medium distance intervals, other races (in which you hope to do well, but you don't make such big allowances in your training schedule to peak for them) and very long training rides.

I used a similar pattern in the work-outs for a first criterium. Those schedules address the generic rider; as you get to know your own performance during your first racing season, you'll be able to fine-tune a peaking programme to shore up your competitive weaknesses. Make sure you taper off to some nice flower-picking touring the week before the race. That will leave you lean and hungry on race day.

After the Great Race, you might have another week or two of top riding in you. If so, find some other events to ride in. Or it might be time to back off and ride more casually. My body has always made it obvious when a peak was over and I have never had much trouble slacking off. But other riders either never hear the message or choose to ignore it.

There is a risk to peaking in bike races, because they have a big element of chance. You might be in great shape but get a flat tyre, or be stuck behind some slow poke when the winning break zips off the front. For these reasons, many riders tend to enter race after race, even if they don't feel particularly good on race day, and see what unfolds. Sometimes a combination of luck and warm-up miles can turn what felt like an off day into a winning day.

To keep from going stale, top riders take a break from riding in November and December. They'll ride, slowly and casually, three or four times a week, go running, and do other sports activities recreationally. This is also prime season to lift weights. Then in January and February, they do their LSD training. When the first races get underway in March and April, they've already started their hard work-outs.

Your early-season LSD should be almost like the touring schedules in the previous chapter, with the same moderate effort levels.

If you ride as fast as you can in January, you'll just be slower at the real races in July. A national-class racer might ride 200 to 250 miles per week in January; most of us would overtrain at that rate and seek our own optimal mileage somewhere between 125 and 200 miles per week.

The Time Commitment

The deeper you get into racing, the more time you need for training. Road racers can't have many other hobbies! But what if you just can't put that much time into riding?

Earlier, I said a rider with little time to train could be able to race short criteriums successfully. That's true, although that rider's time on the bike would have to be pretty intense. Not all of us are cut out for that, mentally or physically.

MOTORPACING

Here's something counter-intuitive to the engineering-minded rider: you can race faster (which, as always, means higher power output) by drafting a motorcycle in training. Why not just train at whatever top speed you can maintain without the motorcycle? With motor pacing, it is easier to hover right at your anaerobic threshold. The motorcycle's wind shadow neutralizes wind gusts and gets you keyed to a higher speed than you'd ever dream of otherwise.

A good motorpacing work-out is a long, steady, extremely brisk ride on flat roads with one to three cyclists—the wind shadow deteriorates if you have more riders. The motorcyclist should sit bolt upright, or stand if he can, to provide maximum wind shadow. He watches his rear view mirror and speedometer to select a speed that's barely aerobically tolerable for you and your companions. Do your 50- and 60-milers this way. You'll come home in record time, fried nonetheless, and ride faster because of it.

Don't motorpace behind a van or car. It is recklessly dangerous. Should the driver be forced to brake suddenly, you'll all pile up on his bumper. Cars can stop much shorter than bicycles, because the limit of their stopping distance is tyre adhesion, not pitchover, and they have lots of tyre to adhere with. Don't ever motorpace behind any four-wheel vehicle, even if you did see the tractor-trailer scene in *Breaking Away*.

Motorpacing involves a friend with a motorcycle (though for most of us, even a moped is fast enough). Make sure your motorcycle driver knows cycling well enough to lead a group of cyclists safely.

If you don't know any motorcyclists who find 25 mph thrilling, you might find some strong tandem riders you could draft. A tandem has twice the horsepower for the same frontal area as a single bike, and it goes about 15 per cent faster. Moreover, a tandem has a great wind shadow.

RACING WITHOUT SPENDING

Bike racing has the image of being an expensive sport. Top riders give interviews saying they have a garage full of bikes which cost a fortune. But you can race on a budget. You can't race for free, but you don't need a second mortgage.

The first thing you need to know is that the difference between a basic bike and a de luxe bike is astonishingly slight. Cheaper bikes used to be made from heavier steels, have sluggish steering geometry, and components unsuitable for competition. All those factors have been fixed in recent years. Basic quality racing bikes are ready to race, right out of the box. The frame geometry and the metallurgy mimic those of far more expensive bikes. So do components.

Expensive bikes have more durable, longer-lasting components with additional features for easy maintenance and adjustment. In some cases, the expensive bike's steering geometry is quicker and less stable—a matter of personal preference and not, as some people claim, an attribute that improves the bike's racing performance. But these things are icing on the cake.

It is essential that your bike has lightweight wheels. At medium-level prices, you'll get lightweight wired-on tyres. Use them for your entry into racing. Tubular tyres, which are standard equipment only on the most expensive models, offer lighter weight (although the gap narrows each year) at greater cost and more maintenance headaches. The time you spend fussing with your tubulars can cut heavily into available training time.

Lightweight frames are made in alloy steel, aluminium, and carbon fibre. Personal preference is the biggest factor in making a choice. Study the specs and decide what properties will best serve you. Bear in mind, though, that alloy steel is well understood and reliable, and still makes the fastest bike for many riders.

The country of national origin matters not

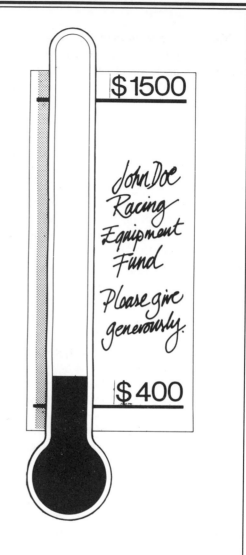

$1500

John Doe Racing Equipment Fund Please give generously.

$400

at all. There used to be a fad among American riders who seriously believed that Italian bikes were so special that you needed one to be competitive. I've never found this, and I've ridden and written road tests of more than 100 racing bikes from at least nine different countries, including about a dozen Italian bikes. Some Italian bikes have been excellent, but no better than or different from the best British, French, Japanese, German, or American bikes I've ridden. There is no Stradivarius-style magic.

Many of my friends like track racing partly because the training time commitment is moderate. The work-outs are absolute killers, but they don't take long. And racing night can be a weekly dose of fun and excitement at a well-run velodrome.

I have work and home obligations that often reduce my on-bike time to less than I would like. In recent years, I've deliberately given up racing so I wouldn't feel pressured to ride when I couldn't, and so I could relax and enjoy the rides I did take, even though I felt out of shape. Many of my friends have followed the same path; others have made sure their lives are carefully structured so they always do have the time to train. The choice is yours.

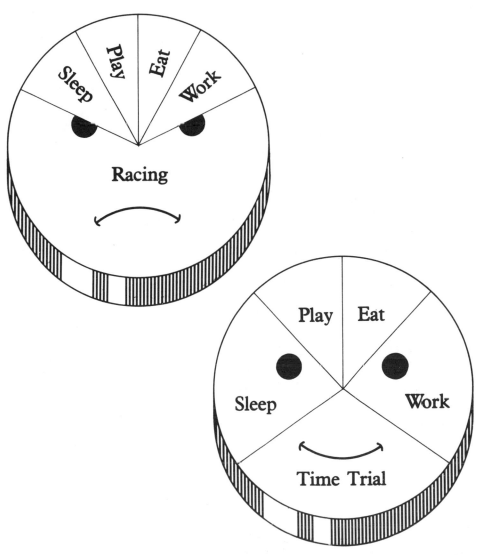

The Great Indoors

Contents

Rolling Through the Winter

Riding a bike is a dubious thing to do when it's frosty winter. Many riders pedal through snow and ice and and think it's reasonably safe, but I'm not one of them. I worry too much that I'll encounter a motorist who has lost his traction to say nothing of me losing mine. It may be sleeting and yucky. It may be just too cold for your personal limit. Or you might not want the neighbours to wonder about your sanity.

A medium-size industry has grown up around the fact of inclement weather, offering all sorts of indoor pedalling devices.

Stationary exercise machines and wheels range in price from cheap to the computer-controlled digital-calorie-burn-rate-readout sky. Some of the cheap ones are awful: tippy, creaky, with felt brake pads lightly gripping a rim, and they vibrate when you pedal. They feel like treacle pudding, particularly at the dead spots in your pedal stroke.

The computer gadgets fitted to indoor pedalling devices are so much health club razzle-dazzle. They give you a meaningless readout in miles per hour and sometimes tell you how many calories you've burned. However, some of the computers set up little work-out games for you, which is worthwhile.

The better exercise machines, such as Sweden's Monark, are rugged and will withstand years of abuse and corrosive sweat. Heavy flywheels make the pedalling action feel like a regular bike's and the work-load is adjustable. Yet most of them, even the Monarch, aren't equipped for cyclists. You have to throw away the pedals, handlebars and seat, and put on real bicycle ones.

There is little sense in exercise machines, because the alternatives are less expensive and offer more.

Rollers, my personal favourite, serve as a kind of bicycle treadmill. They are a great way to improve riding technique: a bike is far less stable on rollers than on the road, and

SWEATING UP A STORM

The room where you're training may be a chilly 45-degree basement, but you'll sweat up a storm anyway. Without the wind to cool you off or make the sweat evaporate, sweat collects on your skin and leaves quite a puddle on the floor underneath your trainer. I get a T-shirt soaking wet in 20 minutes, if I bother to wear one.

This presents two problems: one, the sweat can be harmful to your bike, and two, you may want a breeze to cool yourself off, particularly if you're doing this in a warmer room.

Don't ignore the effect sweat has on your bike. It can cause significant damage, causing the stem to get stuck inside the steerer tube, the headset threads to rust in place, and the paint to blister badly.

The old-fashioned solution was to wrap a T-shirt or towel around your handlebar stem to protect the stem and headset, and any handy plastic on the top tube to protect the paint. (Sweat gets into the brake cable guides and causes the paint to bubble.) The more elegant solution is a new terrycloth product which clips on the handlebars and saddle nose, and protects this area. Make sure you use one of these solutions.

For your own sweating needs, some of the fancier wind trainers have ducted fans, which direct cooling air on your face and chest. Or you can use a small electric fan.

Monark exercise machine

this forces you to become smooth and fluid.

Wind trainers, which probably outsell rollers by ten or 20 to one, are stands which hold the bike upright with outrigger feet. No balancing act is necessary. The rear wheel drives a squirrel cage fan, which churns air and makes you work harder. Some wind trainers use large freewheels to mimic the momentum of your body mass on the road, so the pedalling loads are more similar to those on the road.

A new variant is the magnetic trainer, which uses the resistance of a metal disc spinning in a magnetic field, instead of a fan, to cause resistance. It's far quieter than the wind trainer.

Whatever you do, avoid the false economy of cheap equipment; buy reputable brands from qualified bike shops and you'll be happier.

Choosing and Using Rollers

Rollers help you develop exquisite riding skills. Any awkward motion on your part is magnified by the rollers, forcing you to ride very smoothly just to stay upright. Thus, your steering will be silky smooth, your body motionless from the hips up, and you'll learn to maintain a higher cadence without getting choppy. Sprinters like to train themselves to pedal smoothly up to 180 rpm. The people I know who can do that taught themselves on rollers.

The virtue of rollers is also their undoing. No rider has the skill to handle rollers first time up. If you try some rollers out in a store, you'll probably hate them, and may even fall off and damage your ego. Good news: when you fall off rollers, even if you're pedalling madly, you won't go anywhere. The bike doesn't have any momentum, and the wheel momentum is too small to matter. All you do is slowly topple sideways. Nonetheless, you can become fairly comfortable in one 30-minute practice session, and feel quite at home after five or ten work-outs.

Rollers are often criticized because they don't offer high pedalling loads. And that's

Rollers

somewhat true—they don't simulate the intense resistance of very high speeds, and they don't feel like hill climbing at all. Reading this you'd think it was effortless to spin out your top gear on rollers. Not so. You need to be in pretty good condition to do that. If you're a bit stale, if you're doing other sports in the winter, and if you're using rollers to just keep your sea legs under you, you won't complain about the amount of resistance available.

In other words, that criticism is absolutely true for the racer in shape or the strong tourist. For most others, it's a half truth.

Moreover, at least three companies offer rollers with fans or magnetic resistance units. You can attach or detach the fan belts as you please, in seconds. Then you indeed get the best of all worlds. To my mind, these are the best indoor training devices.

You can also buy a fan that fits atop your rear wheel, for use with any brand of rollers.

Here's how to get comfortable with rollers:

First of all, put them where you have something solid to lean on or grab on either side. A narrow hallway is ideal. I have a solid wall on one side, and a heavy, solid desk on the other. Do not use a chair. When you're first learning rollers, you may need to lunge at your handhold, and a chair will simply topple over when you do that.

Some riders use a doorway. That's not quite as desirable. You need to aim your hands carefully to hit a doorjam each time. A solid floor is essential. Rollers make the whole house vibrate.

Adjust the rollers to your bike's wheelbase. Set the rear wheel in the paired rollers, and adjust the front roller so it's directly under the front axle.

SPRINT IN THE BREAKS

Four walls get boring fast, and you need something to stimulate your mind. What works best?

I have an old black-and-white TV in the cellar and sometimes watch the news while riding rollers. That works reasonably well, although the TV needs to be turned up to top volume to compete with the din of the rollers. When I was beginning on the rollers, I couldn't divert enough attention to follow a TV programme. That came with practice.

It's difficult to watch a film on rollers, because the attention span required to follow the plot is a bit much. Sometimes the rollers demand your attention right when the clue to the murderer's identity is flashed on the screen. Watching films on a trainer is more feasible, but you need either a loud TV or a quiet trainer.

(Americans, as ever, have a new product to solve the problem. Cycling videotapes offer your choice of scenic, rolling country roads, hard-charging pelotons, or programmed indoor work-outs.)

Personal stereos were made for indoor riding.

I've read many a magazine while pounding a Monark at the office. That approach works pretty well. When your effort level is high, at your anaerobic threshold, you won't feel like reading fine print. And the magazines get soaked through with your sweat. But for LSD at a lower effort level, haul out that dog-eared copy of *Ulysses* and go for it!

You can't pay attention to media entertainment during sprint and interval sessions. If you're torn between watching the film and following a work-out plan, I offer this solution: sprint during the commercials or, Walkman fans, during the songs you don't like. Most films have enough commercials to keep your sprint in fine shape.

Don't wear your cleats the first time you try rollers.

Put your bike in a gear around 70 inches and climb on. To get started, lean at a shallow angle so one elbow is resting against the wall and put both hands on the bars and both feet on the pedals. Start pedalling.

Most people tell you to put one hand on the wall or desk and the other hand on the bars. I find that harder, particularly for novices.

With your very first pedal stroke, you'll know you're not on the road. The handlebars want to flop sideways with miniscule steering effort. You'll have to fight the tendency to overcorrect. And body movements you never noticed before will make the bike wobble sideways.

You should be able to balance and bring the bike underneath you right away. It will feel tippy; try not to overcorrect.

Your next task will be to concentrate on staying smooth. When you think you have it wired, try taking one hand off the bars long enough to shift. Not so easy, eh? Give it time and practice.

Rollers come more easily to some people than to others. Even if they come to you slowly, you'll be able to get a useful aerobic work-out after a half-hour of getting to know the rollers. A few hours more, and you'll be comfortable, and you won't feel that they're so all-consuming.

You might even try to go for acrobatic manoeuvres. One of my riding colleagues has mastered the art of sitting up, no hands, and taking his shirt off while he rides—an achievement most of us will never match. He was inspired to do that by Dan Henry, a well-known cycling expert and author who can even take his shorts off, revealing his bikini underwear, while he rides. By the way, Dan Henry is in his 70s.

With continued practice, you'll attain a brisk, smooth roller cadence worth bragging about. That might seem unlikely during your first awkward evening in the cellar, but hang tight: everyone else started on their rollers at 80 rpm, just like you. Improvement comes slowly, one rpm at a time.

Wind Trainers

Wind trainers have evolved nicely since the original Racer Mate appeared at the beginning of the decade. They're compact, easy to install and remove, and available in a range of price/durability levels. They don't teach you to be smooth, but neither do they teach you to be choppy. They're neutral in that regard.

Their resistance is a reasonable simulation of the road. The fancy expensive ones with the heavy flywheels simulate the road more closely. If it's possible to like riding your wind trainer so much that you get fussy about its nuances, this may be a consideration. (A reduced flywheel effect actually simulates climbing, in which the bike can slow down drastically with a big dead spot between pedal strokes.)

The magnetic trainer is appealing because it's so quiet. You can talk in near-normal tones and be heard above it. By contrast, a wind trainer drowns out every other sound. Rollers vary in noise level, but most models are very audible.

There's no technique to learn to get on a wind trainer. Just follow the assembly instructions, plop your bike on, and start pedalling work-outs such as the ones described below. It's the rare rider who finds indoor pedalling entertaining. Even the dullest road through flat agricultural land is a panoply of sensory excitement compared to the four walls of your makeshift basement spa.

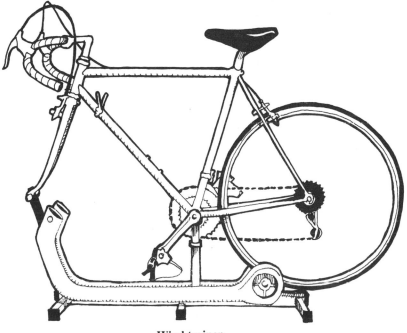

Wind trainer

To ride indoors, you need to be motivated, and you need to plan work-outs that you can tolerate. For most people that means brief sessions that keep your mind occupied with power and sprint training.

Theoretically, indoor riding allows you to a get a jump on your competitors. While they're out jogging in February's sleet, you calmly log your LSD miles in three-hour sessions downstairs, enjoying *Casablanca* or TV repeats as a side benefit.

In practice, though, that's not practical for everyone. It's simply too boring. And your rear end starts to hurt after an hour on rollers. It's a balancing act to stand up and ease the pressure, something you do without thinking on the road, so you have a tendency to put too much weight on your rear.

Nonetheless, if you're one of the lucky ones whose psychological make-up permits you to ride long indoor work-outs, use that to the hilt. By the time the roads are clean you can be fully conditioned to burn fat instead of glycogen, and you will have a big jump on other riders.

However, for most of us, shorter work-outs are far more attractive. I often ride a token half-hour which goes against every physiological principle favouring long-duration exercise, but I get bored, and the news only lasts half an hour.

If you possibly can, go for a longer work-out. An hour is deluxe. A good indoor work-out does take less time than a good outdoor work-out.

Your warm-up takes much less time (no traffic, downhills, etc.) and since there are no distractions or hills to shift for, you can get right to your desired effort level and stay there.

Mix things up with some sprints and intervals. Here's a plan you can use with either rollers or a trainer:

● Five minutes easy twiddle warm-up it'll seem like forever.
● Ten minutes at anaerobic threshold. Medium-tall gear.
● Five minutes easy warm-down.
● Fifteen minutes of interval sets: one minute at slightly anaerobic effort, two minutes of brisk effort near anaerobic threshold. Medium-tall gear.
● Five minutes easy warm-down.
● Five minutes of sprint sets: 30 seconds all out, two minutes recovery. Use a low gear so you spin out your legs.
● Five minutes warm-down.

This takes only 50 minutes, but look at all the training effects you get in such a short time-sprints, aerobic power training, and anaerobic power training!

You can plug a work-out like this into the work-out schedules presented earlier in this book, substituting it for a weekday morning work-out. If you do a work-out like this with fervour, you'll need to recover from it even though it's a brief one. The next day you'll just want to plod along at a brisk aerobic pace and watch the news.

You roller fans will want to see how fast you can spin. I do this by counting my pedal strokes during 30-second sprints. My personal best is 79 pedal strokes (158 rpm). With one fan attached and in the same gear, my sprint drops to 120 rpm.

No harm in trying spin work-outs on the wind trainer, either!

Sprint/interval cocktail
5 minutes warm-up, 10 minutes at anaerobic threshold, 5 minutes warm-down, 15 minutes
interval sets alternating 1 minute slightly anaerobic/2minutes near anaerobic
threshold, 5 minutes warm-down, 5 minutes sprint sets 30 seconds
all out/ 2 minutes recovery, 5 minutes warm-down.

Cross Training

Contents

To Everything There Is a Season

Mankind does not live by pedals alone.

Many cyclists feel they have to take a loyalty oath to the sport, actively eschewing any other kind of exercise. That's a mistake. There is too much fun to be had doing other things. I view cycling as only one of many enjoyable exercises.

Why would you cross train?

● To train for a biathlon or triathlon.

● To take advantage of one sport when another isn't available (e.g. not being able to cycle on business trips or during bad weather).

● To develop physical strengths you don't get from cycling.

● To keep exercising, even though an injury keeps you from your primary sport.

● To enjoy the variety.

If your goal is to be a top competitive cyclist, however, you have to be picky about the exercise you do. US Olympic gold medallist Rebecca Twigg Whitehead, like any top rider, even avoids walking more than short distances during the racing season. The walking motion tightens up her leg muscles and hurts her pedalling style. Top riders spend so much time and energy training specifically for cycling, and need so much time to rest, that alternate exercise detracts from their cycling.

To be a faster cyclist, you need to ride a bike. Some weight and stretching exercises may help with specific problems, and any aerobic exercise builds your cardiovascular system, but only riding a bike really turns the trick. Running, for example, trains all the wrong leg muscles, and causes that tightness that top riders have to avoid.

That said, the same Rebecca Twigg Whitehead spent one winter off-season using running as her main exercise, and she won a world championship gold medal in the pursuit the following summer.

To every thing there is a season. Sometimes you need variety more than you need additional training in a sport you're getting tired of. And most of us don't need to be as picky as the world-class riders. We'll enjoy the variety of doing what we feel like doing more than we'd enjoy the improvement in our cycling.

The first thing you'll notice about cross training is that actively training for two sports at once takes lots of time. Suppose you want a weekly schedule mixing 25 miles of running with 100 miles of riding. That's four hours of running, seven hours of cycling, and about ten hours of getting dressed, showering, pumping up your tyres, and the like. Add, by optimistic estimate, three hours for necessary relaxing and additional sleep, and you have a 20-hour per week part-time job. If you're a triathlete and you toss in swimming, or if you have an active weight programme to boot, you have a big time commitment.

The wrong way to meet your weekly mileage goals is to do each sport equally each day. Instead, have a hard work-out in one sport, and a token work-out or none at all in the other. The next day, trade places.

Good biathletes and triathletes try to minimize the time problem by having vastly unequal training, getting most of their aerobic training from one sport and just some high-quality sharpening work-outs from the other one or two. If you're competing, do most of your training in your slowest sport to speed it up, and try to maintain your ability in the other sports with short, brisk work-outs.

Dead lift

Some people avoid the training time quandary by specializing in different sports at different times of year. By doing that, you can enjoy the variety without the time commitment. The downside is that each time you switch, you go through the soreness of introducing your muscles to a new sport.

What about incompatible muscle training? Cycling, swimming, and running (and for that matter, other exercises ranging from tennis to basketball) do three completely different things to the muscles. Swimming muscles are smooth and lanky; running muscles are tight and stringy; cycling muscles are bulging and powerful. This may or may not be a problem for you. Listen to your body and respond to the signals it gives you. Stretching and massage are the two most beneficial things you can do to avoid problems in this area.

Weights

Cycling will not give you upper body strength, and does not require much. However, exercising with weights can be helpful. Some people find they need additional strength so their upper bodies can be comfortable and hold good form with long hours in the saddle. And track riders absolutely need weight training. They need extraordinary leg muscles and stronger arms and back muscles for their explosive standing sprints, and they just won't get that much body strength through riding.

Weight training is an activity worthy of a book unto itself; here I'll concentrate on making weights an adjunct to cycling as a general fitness programme.

Cyclists usually think of weights as an off-season activity, to build strength to be used when they quit the weights for high-season training. But the sad fact is that strength training, like aerobic training, doesn't stay with you after the work-outs stop. According to exercise physiologist James Dolan, studies show that American football players in season can lose 48 per cent of the strength they gain lifting weights off-season. The moral: start in the

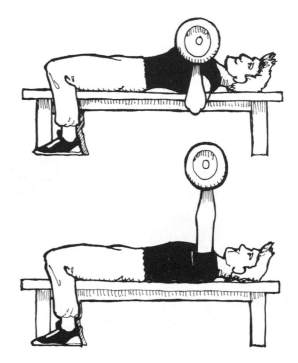

Bench press

off-season when you need an exercise-related distraction. But keep up your programme, or a variant thereof, during the season, too. (One approach: lift three days per week during the off-season, and two days per week during riding season.)

Today, weight training has become the trendy province of the local health club, and that's absolutely the place to learn how to do it. Books are no substitute for having a qualified instructor or coach watch over you and help you avoid injury-producing mistakes in your form.

Make sure your instructor steers you to a programme

Power clean

compatible with your goals. Cyclists (and grocery bag-lifters) don't need huge muscles and lots of brute strength. They need medium-size muscles, and the ability to pump pedals with, perhaps, 150 pounds of force a whole bunch of times. So programmes that emphasize lifting ever-larger weights are not for you. Instead, you'll be better served by lesser weights and greater numbers of repetitions.

Circuit training is well-liked by many cyclists. You do as many repetitions as you can on a particular exercise, then after the 30-second buzzer, abruptly switch to a different exercise for another 30-second bout. There's even a super-aerobic version of this which has you run around the gym, jump rope, or ride a wind trainer for alternate 30-second bouts.

Yet, even circuit training has detractors. It doesn't build massive amounts of strength. Most people can only lift modest weights in circuit regimens, and they aren't able to increase the amount of

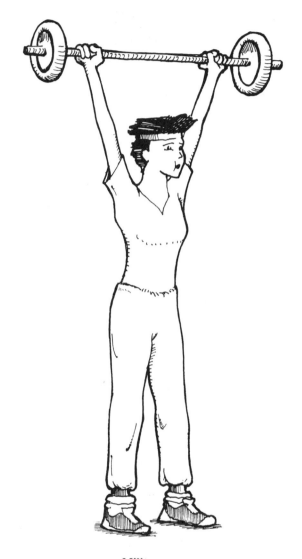

Military press

weight lifted very often. I've been tested before and after a few months of super-aerobic circuit training, and my brute strength, if you could call it that, has increased only slightly. For these reasons, many people prefer slower, more deliberate weight-lifting regimens, saying, 'If you're going to build strength, build strength. Don't try to mix it up with aerobics'.

You'll have to find what works for you. I happen to like circuit training because it makes carrying shopping more comfortable, and it improves my sprint on the bike slightly.

I'm reprinting here a circuit training programme that is unique in its versatility. It's one of the few programmes you can do alone in your basement without a spotter, and without

Squat

having to change the poundage on your weight bar. A basic bog standard weight set is more than ample for this programme.

The programme is from a new book *Weight Training for Cyclists*, by permission of the publisher, Barbara George, and by permission of the author, 1986 US National Veteran Pursuit Champion Andrew J. Buck.

Author Buck, who used this programme himself with obviously positive results, is a busy fellow. He races on the road and track, has a family, and has a job as a college professor. He favours this programme, which he brought to cycling from his former sport, rowing, because he can do it so quickly. He doesn't have time to go to a health club.

The programme originated in the rowing clubs along Philadelphia's Schuylkill River, and is known as the 22-minute drill. Except for warm-up and warm-down, try to do it in 22 minutes. In that time, you do six sets of ten repetitions per set of eight exercises. You never put the bar down, nor do you ever change weights during the exercise. If you meet the 22-minute deadline, you average one lift every two seconds a busy schedule.

Obviously, you use relatively light weights with this drill. Therefore, the risk of serious injury is lessened and the spotter is not absolutely necessary. HOWEVER, if you are brand new to weights, get a friend with substantial weight experience to advise the amount of weight to use, and to talk you through the programme. The only equipment you need besides the barbell is a bench of some kind. I use an old picnic bench covered with towels.

Here are the eight exercises:

1. Deadlift - Start out squatting with the bar on the floor and your hands on the bar a little wider than your shoulders and outside your knees. Stand up, lifting the bar, leaving your arms straight down. As you do the exercise, keep your eyes on the top edge of the wall about 20 feet away. This will keep your back straight and your butt down, essentials for avoiding back injury.

2. Bench Press - Without putting the bar down, move to the bench, lie on your back, and lift the bar smoothly and quickly straight up from your chest.

3. Power Clean - Start out like the deadlift, but in addition to standing up, lift the bar to your shoulders. The bar goes up to your shoulders in one clean motion. Again, it is very important to keep your head up and your butt down. If your butt starts to rise faster than your head, you are inviting disaster. Such a movement puts enormous strain on all the wrong places in your back.

4. Military Press - Hold the bar on your shoulders, behind your head, with your palms facing forward. Lift straight up. Keep your back straight. Let your shoulders and arms do the work.

5. Squat - The bar is already at shoulder height and behind your head, so leave it there while you do your squats. Keep your head up, your back straight, and your butt down as you bend your knees and raise and lower your upper body. Go down until your thighs are

Curls

parallel to the floor, then smoothly go back up. Squats give your quads the strength to sprint, and are considered the backbone of weight training for cyclists. It's easy to hurt yourself doing squats, too. Conventional wisdom has it that you should always, always have a spotter when you do squats, but conventional wisdom has you squatting your body weight if not more. But don't worry; these lightweight squats are still tough. Remember, you do 60 of them in a short time.

   6. Curls - From the standing position at the end of your last squat, bring the bar over your head, lower it until your arms are straight, and reverse your hands so your palms are facing away from you. Bring the bar to your chest, moving only the elbow joint. (Don't cheat by rocking and swaying and heaving the bar.)

   7. Burpee Clean - This somewhat strange exercise is the toughest in the group, partly because it uses muscles still tired from the previous exercises. The burpee clean combines a power clean with a little leg exercise that doesn't involve lifting the bar. After your curls, squat to lower the bar to the floor and rotate your hands so your palms are down, facing you. Still holding onto the bar, thrust your legs out behind you so you're in the push-up

Burpee clean

position. Bring your feet back under you and rise as in a power clean, standing and lifting the bar in one smooth motion. Keep that butt tucked in!

   8. Rows - On the odd-numbered sets, you do the rows standing up straight. On the even-numbered sets, you do the rows bent over at the waist, with your upper body parallel to the floor and your arms hanging straight down.

   In both rows, you hold the bar with your arms straight and your hands about one foot apart, wrists facing you. Lift the bar to your chin. Scratch the bent-over rows if you even think your back objects. It is quite possible to hurt a tired back with that exercise.

   Rowers try to do this work-out with weights of 40-60 per cent of the lifter's body weight. Start out with a very light weight, just to get used to going through the motions. This work-out can really wipe you out if you overdo it.

   What good do you get out of a work-out that uses such light weights? As Buck points out, you get 240 repetitions using the major muscle groups of your legs and lower back, and 240 using various muscle groups in your upper body.

   You can tinker with this work-out to accommodate your objectives. You can use higher weights and ignore the 22-minute time limit to develop greater strength, or you can speed up the work-out and use lower weights for more aerobic benefit. There will always be some aerobic benefit, since you keep moving the entire time and never put the bar down.

Bent-over rows

Do not ever hold your breath or close your eyes when working out with weights. If you find yourself doing either of these, lower the weight on the bar. And don't neglect your warm-up and warm-down. Buck warms up with stretching and calisthenics, then five minutes on the rollers, and warms down with a half hour easy spinning on the rollers.

Vertical rows

Buying a Bike

Contents

Trading Up

Throughout this book, I've assumed that you already own a suitable bike for a demanding rider. But perhaps you don't, or perhaps you have an old heap just begging to be replaced. Or you may want to switch styles of riding. If that's the case, I have some good news: it's a nice time to buy a new bike. Today's bikes, even the medium-price ones, have many improvements in design and materials over bikes from just a few years ago.

Not only that, but the dogs have been weeded from the market-place. In one way, buying a bike is much like buying a stereo or a camera shopping expedition: be prepared to spend at least a week's wages, go to the shop, point to the one whose looks you like, and take it home. In today's marketplace, you can be reasonably well assured that your new possession's quality control, features, and reliability are quite good.

But in another, very important, way a bike is a more complex purchase. Your camera doesn't have to fit your body measurements, or feel comfortable when you're exercising vigorously. Your stereo doesn't care if it's hilly where you live, or how much horsepower you like to deploy to horse over the hills. Neither of them requires regular service.

As high-tech as today's bicycle is, it still should be fitted to your body by the dealer, and it will require some service. It's not like a stereo, which is sold in a sealed box and probably never serviced. Your bicycle must fit your proportions and match your riding style of riding.

If you're buying a replacement for an older bike, you may be able to improve on the way the old one fitted you. Even if you're happy with the fit of the old one, stop and think. You may not know what you're missing. For almost ten years, I didn't enjoy riding as much as I should have because I didn't want to admit I'd bought a bike too big for me. (See the sidebar on 'The Expensive Dimensions' on page 202.)

Because individual fit is so important, a bike shop is one of this world's last bastions of old-fashioned customer service. It's a bit like having a tailor fit a fine suit to your body.

Fit is the most important of several reasons why you should buy only at independent bike shops. Department stores sell lots of bikes, but most of their bikes come in one-size-allegedly-fits-all. Moreover, almost all the bikes they sell are 40-pound gas-pipe specials—not much fun to ride, even if they happen to fit. Department stores are simply not the place to shop for good quality. And most of them provide little in the way of knowledgeable help, parts, service, and accessories.

How much should you spend for a bike? As you pile on those hard-earned pounds, what do you get back in features?

The gateway to good quality begins at about £350, and I suggest you try to budget at least that much if possible. As you move up to £800, there's a steady improvement in features, component quality, durability, and beauty.

Above £800, you start to see diminishing returns. The diminishing starts to get pronounced around £1,000. Bikes do continue to get better up to £2,000 or so, and some owners will be satisfied with nothing less. But that's the stratosphere. Where you fit in this scale is a matter of personal finances and taste, but here's a rough guideline for you to agree or disagree with: the person riding 3,000 miles per year will want a £350 bike. The person riding more than that will want an £500 or £600 bike; the person riding less may find that a less expensive bike fills his needs.

1. Rear derailleur
2. Front derailleur
3. Shift lever
4. Calliper brake
5. Brake Lever
6. Crank set
7. Bottom bracket
8. Hub
9. Pedal
10. Freewheel
11. Chain
12. Headset
13. Seat post

Somewhere above £600 is the threshold of custom bikes. The true custom frame, made to fit your body and none other, is a luxury most of us don't need—but it is easy to want one! The better custom builders have survived the onslaught of the mass manufacturers because their work is so gorgeous. If you have a body of unusual proportions, or you want your bike to be a true work of art, spring for custom.

But if you want value more than beauty, look at the low and medium parts of the price range. You'll be surprised at how many similarities the £250 bike shares with the £500 bike. For example, the lightweight steel frame (described in detail later on) is made from virtually the same double-butted chrome-moly steel tubing. The cheaper bike's frame may weigh a trivial quarter pound more. (Total weight difference between two racing bikes, for example, will be a pound or two—the cheaper bike's components add an ounce here and there.)

Moreover, the cheaper bike will probably have all the knicknacks of the more expensive bikes—brazed-on bosses for multiple water bottles, click-stop index shifting, quick-release brakes. It goes without saying that the cheaper bike will be getting lightweight aluminium components throughout—rims, crankset, handlebar stem, etc.

Racing, Touring, or What?

Most bikes fall in one of the following categories: racing, touring, sport touring, and mountain bike. Your price range will affect your selection.

At the basic price level, the selection is mostly sport touring bikes (hybrids between racing and touring bikes, with medium-weight wheels and medium-range gearing), and entry-level, gentle-use-only mountain bikes.

You have to spend more to get a broader selection. Bullet-proof mountain bikes cost more because of their more painstaking construction, touring bikes more because of the extra brazed-on bosses and wide-range gearing, and racing bikes because the racing bike customer generally likes a flashy bike and insists on spending more.

The sport touring bike is an excellent choice for the fitness-minded person just getting into cycling. Your initial outlay is modest, and yet the only significant difference between today's short-wheelbase sport touring bike and a racing bike is the lighter weight wheels on the racing bike. (Whatever they tell you about the unique handling qualities or climbing ability of the racing frame is so much bunk.)

Lightweight racing wheels are a mixed blessing for the new rider. They're more fragile than touring wheels. You might do well to buy the sport touring bike and hone your bike handling skills on the more durable wheels.

When you want the improved performance of the racing wheels (and you will easily notice the difference), buy a second pair of wheels. Keep your old wheels for backup use, rainy days, or riding on rough roads. A competent dealer can ensure that your new wheels interchange with the old ones instantly, with no derailleur adjustments necessary.

Despite these undeniable truths, most riders prefer the racing bike with its light wheels. The bike feels more spry. Another difference the new rider should note: entry-level racing bikes come with medium-range gearing, so climbing hills remains possible. Expensive racing bikes have narrow-range gearing; only good riders can horse those gears over steep hills. But gears can usually be switched when you are buying the bike.

The touring bike, with its wide-range gearing and wide tyres, was until recently thought of as a breed that had peaked with most manufacturers reducing the number of models on offer. Thanks to the surge in popularity of mountain bikes with their go-anywhere qualities, touring bikes have undergone a re-appraisal and many of the items of equipment offered on mountain bikes—cantilever brakes, Biopace chainrings—are now offered on some pricier touring bikes and sales are increasing all the time. Mine belongs to a previous generation, but nonetheless like all touring bikes, it remains a versatile, useful bike; I like to use mine for exploring because it's comfortable over steep hills and rough roads.

Touring bikes used to come with extra-long wheelbases, to try to fit most of the rider's baggage between the axles. That's no longer considered necessary, because most of the load is carried in front panniers, mounted on the front fork. Lengthening the wheelbase makes no difference when your load is tied to the front fork.

Mountain bikes offer the clearest alternative. For casual round-the-neighbourhood riders they have largely replaced sport touring bikes because the upright riding position and fat tyres are more comfortable. But don't think it's only a luxury bike. You can get quite a work-out, flogging yourself on forestry roads and trails.

Mountain bikes have evolved considerably in design since the first ones were mass-

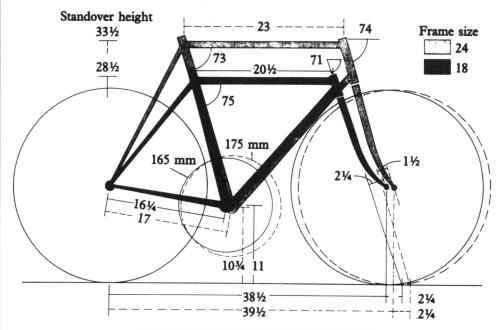

Standover height 33½ 28½

23   74

Frame size
☐ 24
■ 18

73   71   20½   75   175 mm   165 mm

16¼   17

1½   2¼

10¾ 11

38½   2¼
39½   2¼

MATCHING SIZE WITH SHAPE

Frames sized to two people who are a foot apart in height differ substantially in size and shape. These drawings give you an idea how a typical frame for a 5'2" rider differs from a frame for someone 6'2".

Some important differences between the two sizes:

The larger frame has a shallower seat tube angle (73 degrees) and the smaller frame a steeper seat tube angle (75 degrees). Taller riders have longer thighs, and the difference in angle allows optimum positioning over the saddle for both riders.

Similarly, the larger frame has slightly longer chainstays to maintain optimum weight distribution. Few framebuilders actually do this, although it's a nice touch.

The smaller frame's bottom bracket height is higher, not because the rider wants it that way, but because a low bottom bracket would cause the down tube to interfere with the front wheel. This raises the standover height—an unavoidable consequence. The larger frame's 74-degree headtube angle is quite steep, providing quick steering and not

much shock absorption. A shallower head tube angle would give more mellow handling, but then the wheelbase would be too long and the front/rear weight distribution would be poor.

The smaller frame has a shallow 71-degree head tube angle, providing exceptionally stable steering geometry at the expense of some manoeuvrability. Here again, the motive is not rider preference—it's frame geometry. The shallow head tube angle is necessary to provide a long enough wheelbase to avoid overlap between the toe clips and the front wheel.

The larger frame's 23-inch top tube is selected because it will fit the most riders. The smaller frame's 20-inch top tube will provide a good fit for many riders, but many would like it shorter. A shorter top tube would necessitate toe clip overlap or an even shallower head tube angle. Many companies now offer short frames with 24-inch front wheels, so they can size the top tube considerably shorter than you see here.

produced in 1982. Now they have slightly narrower tyres and shorter wheelbases, not to mention better-designed components throughout.

What to Look For

A bicycle has a long list of components, and every one of them improves as you spend more money.

Frames

As I stated earlier, the performance gap between mid-priced and expensive frames has narrowed to a sliver in recent years. Manufacturers almost always use chrome-moly alloy steel, a high grade of steel used for your more exotic household possessions—hand tools, springs, aircraft frames. It's no lighter than humble lawn chair steel, and no more rigid. But it's far stronger. So you can use less of it (in tubes with thinner walls), and still have a frame that won't fall apart from ordinary use.

A lightweight chrome-moly road frame weighs between four and five pounds, depending on frame size, plus another one and three-quarter pounds for the fork, and it

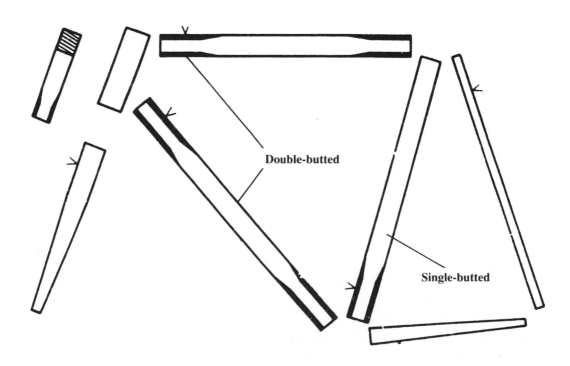

Double-butted

Single-butted

feels lively and resilient on the road. A mountain bike frame will be about a pound heavier because of its beefier tubing. (By comparison, a department store bike frame will have another three pounds of road-hugging weight, and more of a sand-in-the-tyres feel when ridden.)

Tubing is double-butted or triple-butted. That means the wall thickness varies—something only visible inside the tubing. The traditional standard for double-butted racing frames is to have a 0.9 mm wall thickness at each end of the tube, tapering to 0.6 mm in the middle of the tube—pretty thin stuff! (A triple-butted frame has butts of different thicknesses, e.g. 0.9/0.6/0.8 mm.)

Your bike may have Japanese, Italian, or American chrome-moly tubing (or French and English steel alloys that match chrome-moly performance through a different metal-lurgical approach) in the three main tubes.

This cheaper bike may economize by using carbon manganese steel tubing (with walls 0.1 mm thicker to compensate for its lesser metallurgy) in the forks and rear triangle. The resulting performance difference is too slight to discern on the road, and, according to Tange's tubing catalogue, the weight penalty is 120 grams—equivalent to a quarter-full water bottle.

In the basic price range, you'll see frames of carbon manganese and similar steels. Again, tube manufacturers usually increase the wall thicknesses by 0.1 mm over chrome-moly frames. These frames weigh roughly a pound more than their thoroughbred brethren, and they perform quite well.

Frame detailing improves with price. At mid-range, you get forged drop-outs, which make wheel removal and replacement easier. More expensive frames use cast lugs and fork crown; cheaper frames use ones stamped from sheet steel. Cosmetic file work starts to appear around £500.

THE AUTHOR'S STABLE

People asking me for bike-buying advice often ask: 'Well, what do you ride?' By popular demand, here's the Schubert basement inventory:

Our flagship is a 1981 Santana tandem. Faster than any single, set up for long-distance touring, with 27x1.375 touring tyres and gears from 25 to 112 inches, the Santana takes us on our biannual inn-to-inn touring holidays and many other outings.

My touring bike is one of the first (1983) Cannondale aluminium bikes. I set it up for estate car duty with racks, mudguards and (during winter) a Velo-Lux lighting system. I do an occasional solo tour on it, but its customary use is for late-afternoon rides (I turn the lights on before I get back home), exploring half-surfaced country roads within a 20-mile radius, and any ride when I feel lazy and want low gears to fall back on.

My racing/training bike is a 1983 Peugeot PGN-10. It cost less than £200, and it performs quite well. (I lent it to a friend who came back marvelling that it rode just like his £1,000 Colnago.) Since I have relatively little money tied up in it, it's the bike I abuse, riding through late-winter gloppy roads and the like.

My Sunday best bike—technically a racing bike, but given the odds of crashing, any racing I do will be on the Peugeot—is a custom Bruce Gordon (1986). It has quicker handling and a more spry ride than the Peugeot, but the real reason I bought it was that it looked so good. I couldn't stand the thought of not owning it.

My mountain bike is a 1983 Univega Alpina Uno. It was a good bike for its time, but the new Alpina Unos are far, far nicer, for about the same price.

Hanging in the corner, no longer used, is my 1972 Motobecane Le Champion. I have too many happy memories to sell it, but its frame is three inches too big for me.

THE BIG SHOP

When you shop for a motorcycle, you can count the major companies on the fingers of one hand. When you shop for a camera, you need your fingers and toes. Now shop for a bicycle, and you will need several barefoot friends to count all your options! You know what they say about competition. You the customer are in the driver's seat.

The bike industry is intensely competitive, and that simple fact has driven prices down. Years ago at least a month's income was required to buy a plain utility bike; today a week's income is sufficient—and the bikes are considerably better.

With most bikes either imported or assembled here with imported components, the bicycle industry in the UK is especially vulnerable to the fluctuations of sterling on the world currency market. The challenge from the Far-East where the Yen and the Taiwanese dollar have strengthened during the past decade and the failure of European component manufacturers to rival the SunTours and Shimanos in innovation has meant that component prices have risen. But the bite is relatively small, and it's been largely masked by technical advances such as index shifting. Nonetheless bikes continue to be good value.

Another way in which you benefit from the breadth of the bike market is the selection of products available. You have three dozen companies trying to make the bike fit your needs. Want low gears, high gears, or an extra small or extra-large frame? Plain blue or shocking pink? Sealed bearings? A mountain bike also suited for touring, a road bike also suited for gravel, a racing bike also suited for light touring? It's available. And if you want a common bike, such as a sport touring bike or triathlon bike (once known as an 'entry level racing bike'), the selection is intimidatingly vast.

There is a downside to the intense competition in the bike industry: it has skimmed retail profit margins to the point where most retailers must charge extra for special services. If you want component changes at the time you buy the bike, the retailer may well have to charge you for them to avoid losing money. His markups are that slim—particularly when you consider the time he spends assembling the bike, fitting it to the customer, and explaining its many technical details.

The same is true of accessories. If you've just bought an expensive bike, you might expect a couple of free accessories—but that would erase the retailer's profit.

So when you go shopping, you can expect good value. And you can also expect to pay as you go, as your retailer makes his living, a pound at a time.

Perhaps the biggest functional reason to buy the more expensive frame is that you can expect better alignment and machining. Good machining of all the frame's threads, sleeves and faces (for the crank spindle, headset, and seat post) makes it much easier to adjust and replace worn bearings and spindles. One place you can easily see good machine work is the seat tube. On a custom-quality frame, when you loosen the seat post binder bolt a fraction of a turn, the seat post glides down as smoothly as a trombone slide. Tighten it the same fraction and it'll stay put. On a lesser frame, the operation isn't so clean.

As you pay more, you also get more exact tracking and steering alignment. The importance of this is sometimes overrated—enthusiasts talk in thousandths of an inch when it just isn't that critical—but a bike that's in perfect alignment is much easier on the rider over the course of a day-long ride.

Wheels

Make sure the wheels are suited to your style of riding. You'll want the lighter weight and better performance of aluminium rims. (Moreover, they're more dent-resistant than steel rims; steel rims have a much thinner wall thickness at the point where they might meet the road.) Aluminium rims have driven steel rims off the market except in the cheapest bikes.

You'll have to make your own decision about whether to go with racing wheels or the more stout touring wheels. One thing that may surprise you, though, is how small the size differences are. A racing rim will usually be between 19 and 21 mm wide; a touring rim,

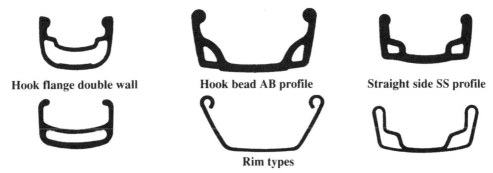

Hook flange double wall   **Hook bead AB profile**   **Straight side SS profile**

Rim types

23 to 25 mm; a mountain bike rim, 27 to 32 mm. The corresponding tyres vary widely, and the only thing you can count on is that their measured width will be narrower—usually about a quarter-inch narrower than the nominal designation (1, $1^1/_8$, $1^1/_4$ inch, or 25, 28 and 32 mm).

On lower-priced bikes, the tyres will be mediocre imitations of the exquisite £25 replacement tyres you see advertised. On more expensive bikes, the tyres will closely mirror the better replacement tyres. The key difference: the cheaper tyre's sidewalls will be thicker. A thin, flexible sidewall will make the tyre more compliant over bumpy road surfaces, and 'sing' better on smooth roads, but it costs more money to make a thin sidewall durable. This is true of mountain bike tyres, too; the most expensive and desirable tyres have very compliant sidewalls. On road bikes, too-thick tread and raised centre ridges make the tyre feel less responsive.

The hubs on any decent bike are forged from a single piece of aluminium—a good, durable construction method.

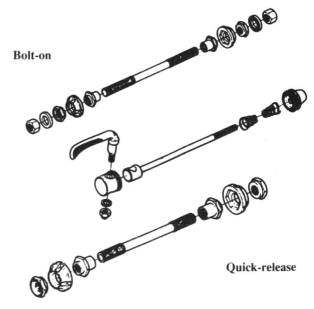

Bolt-on

Quick-release

On decent bikes, you can expect quick-release mechanisms on the front and rear hubs. Quick-release is a wonderful convenience, but if you're buying it for the first time, do yourself a favour: learn how the mechanism works! You should understand the mechanism so thoroughly that you can remove the skewer from the hub, point out all the parts and what they do, and reassemble it. If you don't understand it, you can't attach a wheel safely.

One important feature is, unfortunately, hard to shop for because the sales people have no way of knowing if the bike has it. Better hubs have axles of chrome-moly steel; cheaper hubs use carbon steel axles. Carbon steel axles can bend under rough use. Generally, you can expect chrome-moly axles on mid-price bikes; basic bikes sometimes lack them. There is a bright side: axles are cheap and easy to replace with better ones.

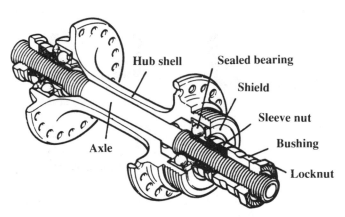

Expensive hubs on £600-plus bikes have exquisitely smooth bearings, but you only feel that when you're playing with them. On the road the differences vanish. Many manufacturers offer sealed hubs; some put rubber seals on their traditional cone-and-cup bearings; others use sealed cartridge bearings. I'm partial to cones and cups because they'll keep running after you've bent an axle, but today's cartridge bearing models have rugged axles and excellent reliability records.

Crankset

The crankset, the most expensive single component on the bike, comes in several forms. On bikes of decent quality you'll find only aluminium cotterless crank sets. These cranks are lighter and more reliable than steel-cottered cranks.

The cheapest ones are cast aluminium. On a bargain basement model, the right crank may be swaged to the chainwheel mounting spider. (On better models, the crank and spider are forged or cast into a single piece of metal.)

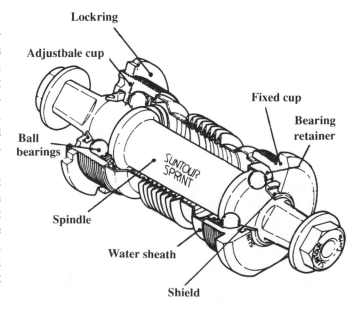

More expensive cranks are forged—a more expensive manufacturing process which traditionally makes a stronger product, but recent advances in casting technology have largely erased that difference.

The more you spend, the greater the availability of different chainwheel sizes and crank arm lengths. The chainwheels will be made from a harder alloy, and they'll last longer. Often, their tooth profile will be fancier, resulting in better shifting. The spindle bearings will feel smoother in your fingers (although the difference can't be felt when your feet are the point of contact). More importantly, the spindle will be more durable.

You'll see a number of out-of-round chainrings on today's market. Shimano has led this trend with the Biopace, a chainring shape that resulted from some very sophisticated human performance testing. The Biopace gives a slight improvement over a round chainring by matching the pedalling effort at each point in the 360-degree pedal revolution to your muscles' ability to exert effort at that point. Sugino's Cycloid and Sakae Ringyo's Oval Tech mimic the Biopace and offer most of Biopace's benefits.

Shimano Biopace

Pedals

The new integrated shoe/pedal systems from Look, Cyclebinding, and AeroLite have stood tradition on its ear. But traditional pedals are what you'll find attached to new bikes.

Good-quality bikes use pedals fashioned out of aluminium castings or forgings. Once again, chrome-moly spindles and smooth bearings are your reward for spending more money. A good pedal will last years.

Pedals come in three distinct styles: quill (the traditional standby), rattrap (the campus model), and platform (for the designer look).

Rattrap pedals are the cheapest; only a few companies make them in good quality models. They're basically metal versions of old rubber-block pedals. Toe clips can be added to most. For mountain bikes, the rattrap has been reincarnated as the beartrap—a

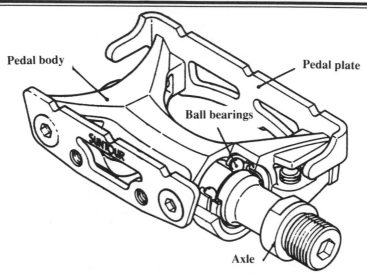

big, beefy pedal with metal teeth to grab the soles of your hiking boots. They're among the very best mountain bike pedals.

Quill pedals, the old standby, cradle your foot between a raised quill on the outside and a lip on the pedal cage on the inside. Unless you have very wide feet, you'll probably prefer the quill pedal over the rattrap pedal.

Platform pedals have been with us for generations, but they're now a popular modern style. A platform pedal has a small platform to hold the front of your foot, a rear cage to support the back of the foot and engage your shoe's cleat, and, usually, non-standard mounting holes for the manufacturer's own unique toe clips. Integrated shoe/pedal systems eliminate the need for toe clips and are popular on racing bikes. They give a stronger more positive attachment than pedals with toe clips, yet can be released whenever the rider requires. They are also, for odd short journeys, easier to use with conventional shoes than pedals with toe clips.

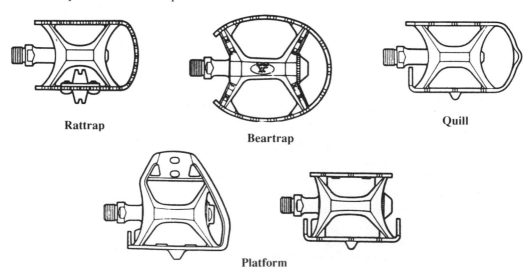

Derailleurs

Now you get to nose around the bike's most intriguing moving part—the derailleur. While the various brands have slightly different personalities, they are all good machines.

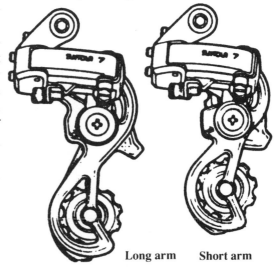

Long arm   **Short arm**

Surprisingly, you don't get better brand-new shifting performance by spending more. The major manufacturers' cheapest derailleurs, even the stamped steel ones that show up on department store bikes, closely copy the designs of the more expensive models. Once again, the differences are found in durability, finish, and the saving of a few ounces with forged aluminium. A good derailleur will work well for many years; a cheap one will wear out with use. A few top-of-the-line models follow a tradition established by Campagnolo—you can replace the pivot bushings and rebuild the derailleur. They last forever.

Rear derailleurs come in versions for narrow-range, medium-range and wide-range gearing; front derailleurs come in narrow and wide varieties. If you're planning to widen the gearing range on the bike you're buying, ask if its stock derailleurs will accommodate your changes. Not only inveterate tinkerers need to consider this; so will a racer who wants to replace the forbidding 21-tooth largest cog with a 24 or 26 for hilly country.

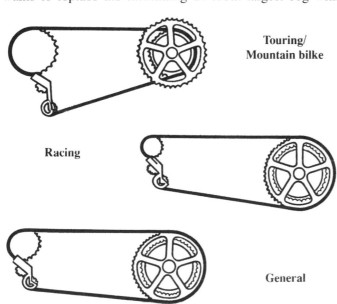

Touring/ Mountain bilke

Racing

General

Some racing rear derailleurs have a maximum cog size of 23 teeth—fine for the flat, not so good for hilly country.

For racers, simplicity is important. There's often little time to shift. Most racing bikes come with an inner chainring of 42 teeth and a large ring of 52 (or, for the one-upsman, 53). Freewheels go 13-18 for flat criterium racing, 13-21 for rolling hills, and 13-24 and 13-26 for steep hills. When you use a bigger freewheel, you compromise the close spacing between gears to get the range you need.

Sport touring bikes gener-

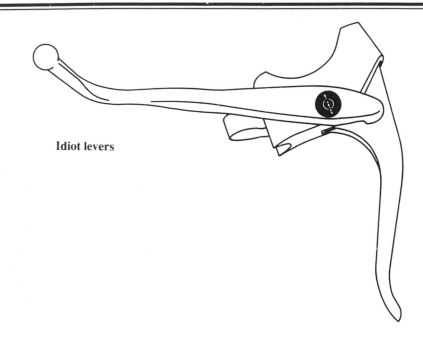

Idiot levers

STRAIGHT TALK ABOUT ASSIST LEVERS

My old boss at the bike shop called them 'idiot levers'. The name stuck. But who's the idiot? Bikes with brake assist levers often outsell bikes without them. Yet the purists who write books and magazines continue to stump against them like the Flat Earth Society, out of synch with the rest.

Brake assist levers look convenient, and they eliminate the task of moving your hands down to the hooks to brake. For riders whose bikes fit so poorly that they can't reach the hooks, the assist levers are the missing ingredient that makes riding possible. (I'd rather banish the people who designed the ill-fitting bike and sold it to that rider, but that's another story.)

Assist levers have a serious downside. With your hands perched on the tops, you're in a miserable position from which to control the bike. Your centre of gravity is too high and your hands are too close together for fine steering control. Your weight is on your seat, and you're poorly positioned to suspend your weight on your hands and feet for maximum control.

When you brake sharply, you need your hands on the hooks, where you can suspend your weight on your limbs and move it down and rearward for better braking performance.

Assist levers don't prevent you from moving your hands to the hooks. But they dissuade you from developing the reflex to move your hands quickly. It's too easy to grab the nearest brake lever. Once you've grabbed the brakes, you're not going to let go!

For these reasons, I urge you to avoid assist levers. If the new bike you're eyeing has them, you can ask the shop to remove them and replace them with rubber hoods on the brake levers. You'll learn to do your 'casual' braking from the tops of the brake levers—a position almost as convenient as the assist lever position. And you'll develop that all-important reflex to move to the tuck position when some serious braking is called for.

ally have milder versions of racing gearing. The chainwheels will be more or less the same, and the freewheel might string from 14 to 26 or 28.

In both cases, you don't get 12 distinct gears. Some small chainring gears will duplicate some large chainring gears. That's okay; the gearing is easy to use and it serves its purpose.

Touring and mountain bike gearing includes much lower gears, so you'll (almost) never have to suffer to pedal up a hill. Hence, you get a large freewheel cog (30 to 34 teeth) and a third, very small chainwheel (between 24 and 30 teeth). The combination allows you to twiddle up a mineshaft at a comfortable four mph.

Derailleurs aren't much good without a chain and freewheel. Better chains from Regina, Sedis, SunTour, and Shimano make the bike shift better; in the basic price range bikes, you may find anonymous chains. In some cases, these no-name chains may hamper the effectiveness of an index shifting system; particular brands of chains, freewheels, and derailleurs are designed to work together.

Freewheels tend to be like water heaters—unexciting, but very reliable. Again, an index shifting system works much better with the correct freewheel.

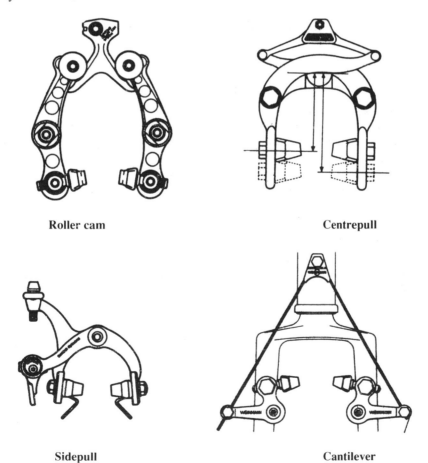

Roller cam   **Centrepull**

Sidepull   **Cantilever**

Brakes

Brakes, you'll be glad to know, are good and durable in the lower price ranges. On bikes mid-price and up, you get improved performance from beefy non-stretch cables and brake pads with more and better friction. Quick-release mechanisms (which spread the brake shoes to allow the tyre past) are usually crude on basic bikes and really nice on mid-price bikes and up. Racing bikes always have traditional sidepull brakes. They're lightweight, they work well, and sidepulls are 'the look'. Touring bikes come with cantilever brakes, largely as a matter of fashion, but sidepulls, which are less ungainly, do an equally good job. Mountain bikes use cantilevers, roller cams, or centrepull-style brakes from Shimano or Dia Compe. Any of these work well.

Why are cantilevers desirable on mountain bikes but less so on touring bikes? A mountain bike needs a brake designed to offer good performance while reaching around fat tyres. Touring bikes have much smaller tyres, and reach is not difficult. They have a different problem: cantilever brakes can sometimes get in the way of panniers. I have sidepulls on my touring bike; they work fine, and they handily reach around both tyre and mudguard.

Headset

There's only one moving part left: the headset. The headset is the set of bearings that allow the fork to pivot in the frame. You want it in perfect condition. If it's not, the bike's handling will suffer. Fancier bikes come with better, longer lasting headsets, installed with more painstaking care so their alignment is good. I've generally found the headsets on £300 bikes adequate, but the ones on more expensive bikes are far easier to get into good adjustment. They go more miles before needing another adjustment. And waterproof bearing seals are a common enticement to spend more.

Saddle

The saddle should feel good, of course, but different butts have different preferences. You'll see saddles that are wide and firm, narrow and cushy, narrow and firm, wide and cushy, with bumps for your buttocks, with dimples for your bottom, with covers, with holes . . . oh, what a choice. Each kind has loyal supporters and rabid enemies. The only way to know which kind you'll eventually prefer is to ride on it.

There are a few constants: First, most women will find the wider women's saddles a real improvement. Women's pelvises are wider than men's, and they're better matched to those wider saddles. Second, everyone's backside needs an adjustment period. I still get a sore butt on the first long ride each spring.

But if the soreness doesn't go away, start shopping. One sure cure: the wonderful elastic gel materials offered by Spenco (as a saddle cover) and Persons-Majestic and Avocet (integrated into the saddle) absolutely eliminate the sore butt. Your last excuse for not riding just disappeared. Enjoy the ride! Cycling is a wonderful lifetime sport. May riding bring you as much pleasure as it brings me

BUYING CLOTHING

If you, like I, wouldn't be seen in a bright pink skin suit, you may wonder what cycling clothing is all about.

The answer: comfort. Counter-intuitive though it may be, those 'spray painted' outfits are the most comfortable thing you can wear on a warm day.

There's a vast selection of clothing. What do you buy first, to get the most function for your money? The answer is easy: a helmet, gloves, and cycling shoes. Virtually any helmet you find in stores to day will meet the crash test of the American National Standards Institute and say so (look for the sticker reading, 'ANSI Z-90.4'). (A BSI standard is still in the works.) That test is a rigorous one, and it ensures that helmets really perform during the millisecond you need them. Gloves keep your hands comfortable on a long ride; cleated shoes, discussed in Chapter 1, multiply your muscle power and actually increase your foot comfort on a long ride.

Your next purchase for summer riding should be shorts. Lycra skin shorts are the most popular, and with good reason: they're the most comfortable. Because they're tight, your skin doesn't gather and pinch underneath them. But in cool weather, cover your legs: below 68 degrees, you'll want to wear Lycra tights; below 50 degrees, heavier wool or polypropylene tights. Your knees will last longer if you keep them warm. When I was an impoverished student, I wore cotton long johns instead of tights. No points for style, but I kept my legs warm.

In hot weather, a jersey offers some improvement over a T-shirt. It's in variable weather, when you may go from cool to warm conditions in a single ride, that the knit jersey becomes far superior. It will keep you comfortable in all conditions, where the T-shirt is only good in warm conditions.

You'll find cotton isn't used much in cycling clothing. The biggest reason is that it soaks up water (whether from sweat or from rain) and becomes clammy and chilly. Wool, the traditional favourite, performs about as well in warm weather but better in cool weather. Polypropylene is wonderfully cool in warm weather and warm in cool weather. No matter how much you sweat, the fabric remains nearly bone dry.

In autumn and spring, wool or polypropylene cycling jackets with nylon windbarrier fabric fronts are the most comfortable thing you can wear. They breathe well, stop the wind chill factor, and their fabric stays dry.

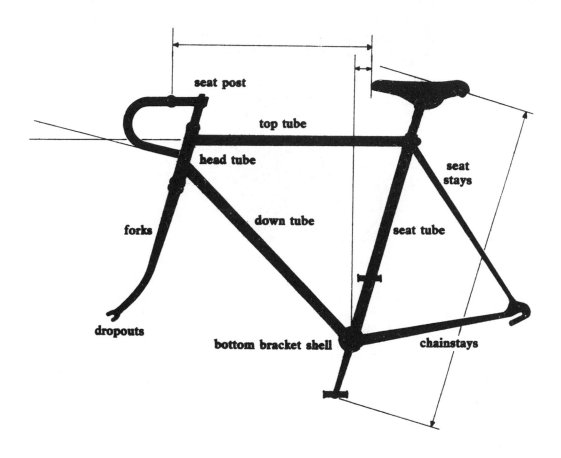

THE EXPENSIVE DIMENSIONS

A seat post can be moved up and down, but when you buy a bike, you commit yourself to some dimensions for good. Here they are, and here's what you should know about them:

Frame size

When you go to buy a bike, the salesman will often ask you to straddle a bike on the showroom floor. If you can do so with your feet flat on the floor, and an inch of clearance between your crotch and the top tube, he'll cheerfully announce that the bike fits perfectly.

Well, there is more to it than that. Because seat posts adjust up and down, more than one frame size will work for you. For example, I

prefer to ride a 21-inch frame (I'm an average-size man with a 32-inch inseam). With that frame size, a standard (180 mm) seat post is extended almost all the way to give me proper leg extension.

But the 'straddle the top tube' test won't necessarily point me to a 21-inch frame, because I can also straddle a frame up to 23 inches. And the two frame sizes behave very differently. The smaller frame feels much, much more manoeuvrable. The larger frame somehow doesn't feel as willing to corner quickly.

These size-induced differences are major, far bigger than the differences you get by buying a more expensive frame. I would rather ride a basic bike with a 21-inch frame than a £2,000 bike with a 23-inch frame.

For these reasons, I recommend that people size their frames like I do—so that they have nearly full extension with a 180 mm seat post. Crotch clearance becomes a moot point (you're bound to have plenty).

If you've been riding a frame that's larger than necessary, you'll find a smaller frame's lively feel and shorter top tube take some getting used to. But when you get used to it, you'll probably prefer it.

There are exceptions. Some riders prefer a larger frame, with less seat post showing, to get a slightly more relaxed ride, mellow handling, and higher handlebar placement. Some riders simply need the bars higher to attain a comfortable position.

For mountain bikes, you'll want a frame two or three inches smaller than your road bike size; a longer seat post provides adequate leg extension.

Handlebar reach

Reach was covered in Chapter 3, and I suggested that you buy a different handlebar stem if necessary. But now you're buying a bike, and you get to pick your top tube length.

Here's where short people with short arms have to stick up for their rights. The handlebars must be close enough so that you can comfortably put your hands on the hooks (where the brake levers are), so you can easily control the bike from this position. Many a short person will find riding far more comfortable on a small bike with a 24-inch front wheel and 19-inch top tube. (The shortest top tubes with 27-inch front wheels are generally 20 inches.) Don't buy a bike you can't ride comfortably!

Tall riders with long arms may find the reach too short on some bikes. The warning sign: when your hands are on the hooks, your upper arms aren't sloping forward at all. If a stem change isn't sufficient, you'll need a longer top tube, which usually means a larger frame size.

Handlebar width

Usually, the handlebar width will be within acceptable bounds for you; handlebars are sized to the bike, and the human body can tolerate some variance. However, if you're very big or very small, take note of the width: drop handlebars range from 36 to 44 cm wide, measured from the centre of one plug to the centre of the other plug. (Most bars on production bikes are between 39 and 42 cm.) If you need extra-wide or extra-narrow bars, you can ask the dealer to make the switch when you buy the bike. It shouldn't cost too much.

On mountain bikes, the preferred width depends on how you will be using the bike. The gonzo downhill riders prefer bars 28 inches wide, to give them extra leverage for better control. However, most riders will prefer narrower bars—26 or even 24 inches. The narrower bars give a more natural feel and better slow-speed manoeuvrability, and their high-speed control is better than most of us will ever need.

Crank length

Crank length is an expensive dimension. Replacement crank arms are upwards of £50 per pair, and few bike shops see enough demand to stock many sizes, brands and models. Most good brands come in 165, 170, 175 and 180 mm. Going from 165 to 180 nets you 15 mm, or 0.6 inch. Given the cost, many people never bother.

But it's sometimes worth it. Riders most likely to feel an improvement are 6-plus-footers who move up from the standard 170s—their long legs feel set free by the 510 mm difference.

Short riders are usually happy with 165s or even 170s. (Cranks feel too small more readily than they feel too large.) If you're short and 165s feel long for you, your bike shop can order French T.A. brand cranks in 160 or even 150 mm.

ALTERNATIVES TO STEEL

Although a steel frame is a well-designed, near-perfect structure, purveyors of aluminium and carbon fibre have made a huge dent in steel's long reign. And they offer frames with qualities not possible in steel.

Briefly, here are the main categories these alternatives fall into:

Oversize aluminium frames, offered by Klein and Cannondale, are several times more rigid than conventional steel frames. They're also considerably lighter—half to one-and-a-half pounds lighter than steel frames of similar dimensions. They're easily recognized by their outsize beer can tubing diameter. It stands out from a steel frame.

The extra rigidity makes the frame absorb much less of your pedalling effort —although since a conventional steel frame absorbs about one half of one per cent of that effort, the difference is more one of feel than a huge improvement in efficiency (as measured in the lab). Nonetheless, many riders vastly prefer the feel of the more rigid frame. It's especially suitable for big, strong, heavy riders, who do flex their frames more than smaller, lighter riders.

Another surprising result is that these ultra-rigid frames track a rough road at least as well as—and in the opinion of many riders, far better than—a steel frame. The aluminium appears to dampen the road shock better than steel, too.

The next category is the largest one. An increasing number of manufacturers make aluminium frames that have approximately the same rigidity as steel frames. Many of their frames weigh another half pound or so less than the Klein/Cannondale category, and some have further weight savings with aluminium forks.

A rider who doesn't require extreme rigidity, but wants weight savings and a further dampening of road shock, may find these frames his best choice.

The third category of frame includes France's Vitus and Italy's Alan. These frames are lighter and more flexible still. For a lightweight, smooth-pedalling rider who spends many hours per day in the saddle, their exceptional shock-absorbing makes them very desirable. Since European professional riders fit that description, many of them have become ardent fans of that frame type. You see it in many of the pro races.

Most carbon fibre frames perform similarly to the Vitus and Alan aluminium frames, perhaps with even more shock absorption. This is bound to change over the next few years, as manufacturers explore carbon fibre's unique properties to make ultra-light, ultra-rigid, and ultra- expensive frames. Already the monocoque Kestral frame is doing that. There will be others like it in the near future.

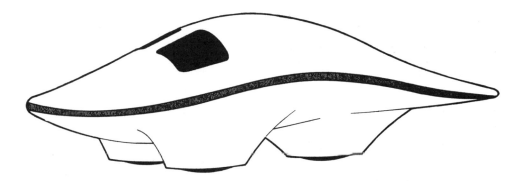

Commuter of the future? *Fusion* **is a four-person, human-powered vehicle clocked in speed
trials at 54 mph plus and capable of average speeds of 30-40 mph on open roads.**

GEAR RATIO CHART FOR 27 INCH WHEELS

Number of teeth on chainring

Cog	24	25	26	27	28	29	30	31	32	33	34	35	36	37	38	39	40	41	42	43	44	45	46	47	48	49	50	51	52	53	54	55	56	57	58
12	54.0	56.3	58.5	60.8	63.0	65.3	67.5	69.8	72.0	74.3	76.5	78.8	81.0	83.3	85.5	87.8	90.0	92.3	94.5	96.8	99.0	101.3	103.5	105.8	108.0	110.3	112.5	114.8	117.0	119.3	121.5	123.8	126.0	128.3	130.5
13	49.8	51.9	54.0	56.1	58.2	60.2	62.3	64.4	66.5	68.5	70.6	72.7	74.8	76.8	78.9	81.0	83.1	85.2	87.2	89.3	91.4	93.5	95.5	97.6	99.7	101.8	103.8	105.9	108.0	110.1	112.2	114.2	116.3	118.4	120.5
14	46.3	48.2	50.1	52.1	54.0	55.9	57.9	59.8	61.7	63.6	65.6	67.5	69.4	71.4	73.3	75.2	77.1	79.1	81.0	82.9	84.9	86.8	88.7	90.6	92.6	94.5	96.4	98.4	100.3	102.2	104.1	106.1	108.0	109.9	111.9
15	43.2	45.0	46.8	48.6	50.4	52.2	54.0	55.8	57.6	59.4	61.2	63.0	64.8	66.6	68.4	70.2	72.0	73.8	75.6	77.4	79.2	81.0	82.8	84.6	86.4	88.2	90.0	91.8	93.6	95.4	97.2	99.0	100.8	102.6	104.4
16	40.5	42.2	43.9	45.6	47.3	48.9	50.6	52.3	54.0	55.7	57.4	59.1	60.8	62.4	64.1	65.8	67.5	69.2	70.9	72.6	74.3	75.9	77.6	79.3	81.0	82.7	84.4	86.1	87.8	89.4	91.1	92.8	94.5	96.2	97.9
17	38.1	39.7	41.3	42.9	44.5	46.1	47.6	49.2	50.8	52.4	54.0	55.6	57.2	58.8	60.4	61.9	63.5	65.1	66.7	68.3	69.9	71.5	73.1	74.6	76.2	77.8	79.4	81.0	82.6	84.2	85.8	87.4	88.9	90.5	92.1
18	36.0	37.5	39.0	40.5	42.0	43.5	45.0	46.5	48.0	49.5	51.0	52.5	54.0	55.5	57.0	58.5	60.0	61.5	63.0	64.5	66.0	67.5	69.0	70.5	72.0	73.5	75.0	76.5	78.0	79.5	81.0	82.5	84.0	85.5	87.0
19	34.1	35.5	36.9	38.4	39.8	41.2	42.6	44.1	45.5	46.9	48.3	49.7	51.2	52.6	54.0	55.4	56.8	58.3	59.7	61.1	62.5	63.9	65.4	66.8	68.2	69.6	71.1	72.5	73.9	75.3	76.7	78.2	79.6	81.0	82.4
20	32.4	33.8	35.1	36.5	37.8	39.2	40.5	41.9	43.2	44.6	45.9	47.3	48.6	50.0	51.3	52.7	54.0	55.4	56.7	58.1	59.4	60.8	62.1	63.5	64.8	66.2	67.5	68.9	70.2	71.6	72.9	74.3	75.6	77.0	78.3
21	30.9	32.1	33.4	34.7	36.0	37.3	38.6	39.9	41.1	42.4	43.7	45.0	46.3	47.6	48.9	50.1	51.4	52.7	54.0	55.3	56.6	57.9	59.1	60.4	61.7	63.0	64.3	65.6	66.9	68.1	69.4	70.7	72.0	73.3	74.6
22	29.5	30.7	31.9	33.1	34.4	35.6	36.8	38.0	39.3	40.5	41.7	43.0	44.2	45.4	46.6	47.9	49.1	50.3	51.5	52.8	54.0	55.2	56.5	57.7	58.9	60.1	61.4	62.6	63.8	65.0	66.3	67.5	68.7	70.0	71.2
23	28.2	29.3	30.5	31.7	32.9	34.0	35.2	36.4	37.6	38.7	39.9	41.1	42.3	43.4	44.6	45.8	47.0	48.1	49.3	50.5	51.7	52.8	54.0	55.2	56.3	57.5	58.7	59.9	61.0	62.2	63.4	64.6	65.7	66.9	68.1
24	27.0	28.1	29.3	30.4	31.5	32.6	33.8	34.9	36.0	37.1	38.3	39.4	40.5	41.6	42.8	43.9	45.0	46.1	47.3	48.4	49.5	50.6	51.8	52.9	54.0	55.1	56.3	57.4	58.5	59.6	60.8	61.9	63.0	64.1	65.3
25	25.9	27.0	28.1	29.2	30.2	31.3	32.4	33.5	34.6	35.6	36.7	37.8	38.9	40.0	41.0	42.1	43.2	44.3	45.4	46.4	47.5	48.6	49.7	50.8	51.8	52.9	54.0	55.1	56.2	57.2	58.3	59.4	60.5	61.6	62.6
26	24.9	26.0	27.0	28.0	29.1	30.1	31.2	32.2	33.2	34.3	35.3	36.3	37.4	38.4	39.5	40.5	41.5	42.6	43.6	44.7	45.7	46.7	47.8	48.8	49.8	50.9	51.9	53.0	54.0	55.0	56.0	57.1	58.2	59.2	60.2
27	24.0	25.0	26.0	27.0	28.0	29.0	30.0	31.0	32.0	33.0	34.0	35.0	36.0	37.0	38.0	39.0	40.0	41.0	42.0	43.0	44.0	45.0	46.0	47.0	48.0	49.0	50.0	51.0	52.0	53.0	54.0	55.0	56.0	57.0	58.0
28	23.1	24.1	25.1	26.0	27.0	28.0	28.9	29.9	30.9	31.8	32.8	33.8	34.7	35.7	36.6	37.6	38.6	39.5	40.5	41.5	42.4	43.4	44.4	45.3	46.3	47.3	48.2	49.2	50.1	51.1	52.1	53.0	54.0	55.0	55.9
29	22.3	23.3	24.2	25.1	26.1	27.0	27.9	28.9	29.8	30.7	31.7	32.6	33.5	34.5	35.4	36.3	37.2	38.2	39.1	40.0	41.0	41.9	42.8	43.8	44.7	45.6	46.6	47.5	48.4	49.3	50.3	51.2	52.1	53.1	54.0
30	21.6	22.5	23.4	24.3	25.2	26.1	27.0	27.9	28.8	29.7	30.6	31.5	32.4	33.3	34.2	35.1	36.0	36.9	37.8	38.7	39.6	40.5	41.4	42.3	43.2	44.1	45.0	45.9	46.8	47.7	48.6	49.5	50.4	51.3	52.2
31	20.9	21.8	22.6	23.5	24.4	25.3	26.1	27.0	27.9	28.7	29.6	30.5	31.4	32.2	33.1	34.0	34.8	35.7	36.6	37.5	38.3	39.2	40.1	40.9	41.8	42.7	43.5	44.4	45.3	46.2	47.0	47.9	48.8	49.6	50.5
32	20.3	21.1	21.9	22.8	23.6	24.5	25.3	26.2	27.0	27.8	28.7	29.5	30.4	31.2	32.1	32.9	33.8	34.6	35.4	36.3	37.1	38.0	38.8	39.7	40.5	41.3	42.2	43.0	43.9	44.7	45.6	46.4	47.3	48.1	48.9
33	19.6	20.5	21.3	22.1	22.9	23.7	24.5	25.4	26.2	27.0	27.8	28.6	29.5	30.3	31.1	31.9	32.7	33.5	34.4	35.2	36.0	36.8	37.6	38.5	39.3	40.1	40.9	41.7	42.5	43.4	44.2	45.0	45.8	46.6	47.5
34	19.1	19.9	20.6	21.4	22.2	23.0	23.8	24.6	25.4	26.2	27.0	27.8	28.6	29.4	30.2	31.0	31.8	32.6	33.4	34.1	34.9	35.7	36.5	37.3	38.1	38.9	39.7	40.5	41.3	42.1	42.9	43.7	44.5	45.3	46.1
35	18.5	19.3	20.1	20.8	21.6	22.4	23.1	23.9	24.7	25.5	26.2	27.0	27.8	28.5	29.3	30.1	30.9	31.6	32.4	33.2	33.9	34.7	35.5	36.3	37.0	37.8	38.6	39.3	40.1	40.9	41.7	42.4	43.2	44.0	44.7
36	18.0	18.8	19.5	20.3	21.0	21.8	22.5	23.3	24.0	24.8	25.5	26.3	27.0	27.8	28.5	29.3	30.0	30.8	31.5	32.3	33.0	33.8	34.5	35.3	36.0	36.8	37.5	38.3	39.0	39.8	40.5	41.3	42.0	42.8	43.5
37	17.5	18.2	19.0	19.7	20.4	21.2	21.9	22.6	23.4	24.1	24.8	25.5	26.3	27.0	27.7	28.5	29.2	29.9	30.6	31.4	32.1	32.8	33.6	34.3	35.0	35.8	36.5	37.2	37.9	38.7	39.4	40.1	40.9	41.6	42.3
38	17.1	17.8	18.5	19.2	19.9	20.6	21.3	22.0	22.7	23.4	24.2	24.9	25.6	26.3	27.0	27.7	28.4	29.1	29.8	30.6	31.3	32.0	32.7	33.4	34.1	34.8	35.5	36.2	36.9	37.7	38.4	39.1	39.8	40.5	41.2

Number of teeth on chainring

GEAR RATIO CHART FOR 26 INCH WHEELS

Number of teeth on chainring

	24	25	26	27	28	29	30	31	32	33	34	35	36	37	38	39	40	41	42	43	44	45	46	47	48	49	50	51	52	53	54	55	56	57	58	
12	52.0	54.2	56.3	58.5	60.7	62.8	65.0	67.2	69.3	71.5	73.7	75.8	78.0	80.2	82.3	84.5	86.7	88.8	91.0	93.2	95.3	97.5	99.7	101.8	104.0	106.2	108.3	110.5	112.7	114.8	117.0	119.2	121.3	123.5	125.7	12
13	48.0	50.0	52.0	54.0	56.0	58.0	60.0	62.0	64.0	66.0	68.0	70.0	72.0	74.0	76.0	78.0	80.0	82.0	84.0	86.0	88.0	90.0	92.0	94.0	96.0	98.0	100.0	102.0	104.0	106.0	108.0	110.0	112.0	114.0	116.0	13
14	44.6	46.4	48.3	50.1	52.0	53.9	55.7	57.6	59.4	61.3	63.1	65.0	66.9	68.7	70.6	72.4	74.3	76.1	78.0	79.9	81.7	83.6	85.4	87.3	89.1	91.0	92.9	94.7	96.6	98.4	100.3	102.1	104.0	105.9	107.7	14
15	41.6	43.3	45.1	46.8	48.5	50.3	52.0	53.7	55.5	57.2	58.9	60.7	62.4	64.1	65.9	67.6	69.3	71.1	72.8	74.5	76.3	78.0	79.7	81.5	83.2	84.9	86.7	88.4	90.1	91.9	93.6	95.3	97.1	98.8	100.5	15
16	39.0	40.6	42.3	43.9	45.5	47.1	48.8	50.4	52.0	53.6	55.3	56.9	58.5	60.1	61.8	63.4	65.0	66.6	68.3	69.9	71.5	73.1	74.8	76.4	78.0	79.6	81.3	82.9	84.5	86.1	87.8	89.4	91.0	92.6	94.3	16
17	36.7	38.2	39.8	41.3	42.8	44.4	45.9	47.4	48.9	50.5	52.0	53.5	55.1	56.6	58.1	59.6	61.2	62.7	64.2	65.8	67.3	68.8	70.4	71.9	73.4	74.9	76.5	78.0	79.5	81.1	82.6	84.1	85.6	87.2	88.7	17
18	34.7	36.1	37.6	39.0	40.4	41.9	43.3	44.8	46.2	47.7	49.1	50.6	52.0	53.4	54.9	56.3	57.8	59.2	60.7	62.1	63.6	65.0	66.4	67.9	69.3	70.8	72.2	73.7	75.1	76.6	78.0	79.4	80.9	82.3	83.8	18
19	32.8	34.2	35.6	36.9	38.3	39.7	41.1	42.4	43.8	45.2	46.5	47.9	49.3	50.6	52.0	53.4	54.7	56.1	57.5	58.8	60.2	61.6	62.9	64.3	65.7	67.1	68.4	69.8	71.2	72.5	73.9	75.3	76.6	78.0	79.4	19
20	31.2	32.5	33.8	35.1	36.4	37.7	39.0	40.3	41.6	42.9	44.2	45.5	46.8	48.1	49.4	50.7	52.0	53.3	54.6	55.9	57.2	58.5	59.8	61.1	62.4	63.7	65.0	66.3	67.6	68.9	70.2	71.5	72.8	74.1	75.4	20
21	29.7	31.0	32.2	33.4	34.7	35.9	37.1	38.4	39.6	40.9	42.1	43.3	44.6	45.8	47.0	48.3	49.5	50.8	52.0	53.2	54.5	55.7	57.0	58.2	59.4	60.7	61.9	63.1	64.4	65.6	66.9	68.1	69.3	70.6	71.8	21
22	28.4	29.5	30.7	31.9	33.1	34.3	35.5	36.6	37.8	39.0	40.2	41.4	42.5	43.7	44.9	46.1	47.3	48.5	49.6	50.8	52.0	53.2	54.4	55.5	56.7	57.9	59.1	60.3	61.5	62.6	63.8	65.0	66.2	67.4	68.5	22
23	27.1	28.3	29.4	30.5	31.7	32.8	33.9	35.0	36.2	37.3	38.4	39.6	40.7	41.8	43.0	44.1	45.2	46.3	47.5	48.6	49.7	50.9	52.0	53.1	54.3	55.4	56.5	57.7	58.8	59.9	61.0	62.2	63.3	64.4	65.6	23
24	26.0	27.1	28.2	29.3	30.3	31.4	32.5	33.6	34.7	35.8	36.8	37.9	39.0	40.1	41.2	42.3	43.3	44.4	45.5	46.6	47.7	48.8	49.8	50.9	52.0	53.1	54.2	55.3	56.3	57.4	58.5	59.6	60.7	61.8	62.8	24
25	25.0	26.0	27.0	28.1	29.1	30.2	31.2	32.2	33.3	34.3	35.4	36.4	37.4	38.5	39.5	40.6	41.6	42.6	43.7	44.7	45.8	46.8	47.8	48.9	49.9	51.0	52.0	53.0	54.1	55.1	56.2	57.2	58.2	59.3	60.3	25
26	24.0	25.0	26.0	27.0	28.0	29.0	30.0	31.0	32.0	33.0	34.0	35.0	36.0	37.0	38.0	39.0	40.0	41.0	42.0	43.0	44.0	45.0	46.0	47.0	48.0	49.0	50.0	51.0	52.0	53.0	54.0	55.0	56.0	57.0	58.0	26
27	23.1	24.1	25.0	26.0	27.0	27.9	28.9	29.9	30.8	31.8	32.7	33.7	34.7	35.6	36.6	37.6	38.5	39.5	40.4	41.4	42.4	43.3	44.3	45.3	46.2	47.2	48.1	49.1	50.1	51.0	52.0	53.0	53.9	54.9	55.9	27
28	22.3	23.2	24.1	25.1	26.0	26.9	27.9	28.8	29.7	30.6	31.6	32.5	33.4	34.4	35.3	36.2	37.1	38.1	39.0	39.9	40.9	41.8	42.7	43.6	44.6	45.5	46.4	47.4	48.3	49.2	50.1	51.1	52.0	52.9	53.9	28
29	21.5	22.4	23.3	24.2	25.1	26.0	26.9	27.8	28.7	29.6	30.5	31.4	32.3	33.2	34.1	35.0	35.9	36.8	37.7	38.6	39.4	40.3	41.2	42.1	43.0	43.9	44.8	45.7	46.6	47.5	48.4	49.3	50.2	51.1	52.0	29
30	20.8	21.7	22.5	23.4	24.3	25.1	26.0	26.9	27.7	28.6	29.5	30.3	31.2	32.1	32.9	33.8	34.7	35.5	36.4	37.3	38.1	39.0	39.9	40.7	41.6	42.5	43.3	44.2	45.1	45.9	46.8	47.7	48.5	49.4	50.3	30
31	20.1	21.0	21.8	22.6	23.5	24.3	25.2	26.0	26.8	27.7	28.5	29.4	30.2	31.0	31.9	32.7	33.5	34.4	35.2	36.1	36.9	37.7	38.6	39.4	40.3	41.1	41.9	42.8	43.6	44.5	45.3	46.1	47.0	47.8	48.6	31
32	19.5	20.3	21.1	21.9	22.8	23.6	24.4	25.2	26.0	26.8	27.6	28.4	29.3	30.1	30.9	31.7	32.5	33.3	34.1	34.9	35.8	36.6	37.4	38.2	39.0	39.8	40.6	41.4	42.3	43.1	43.9	44.7	45.5	46.3	47.1	32
33	18.9	19.7	20.5	21.3	22.1	22.8	23.6	24.4	25.2	26.0	26.8	27.6	28.4	29.2	29.9	30.7	31.5	32.3	33.1	33.9	34.7	35.5	36.2	37.0	37.8	38.6	39.4	40.2	41.0	41.8	42.5	43.3	44.1	44.9	45.7	33
34	18.4	19.1	19.9	20.6	21.4	22.2	22.9	23.7	24.5	25.2	26.0	26.8	27.5	28.3	29.1	29.8	30.6	31.4	32.1	32.9	33.6	34.4	35.2	35.9	36.7	37.5	38.2	39.0	39.8	40.5	41.3	42.1	42.8	43.6	44.4	34
35	17.8	18.6	19.3	20.1	20.8	21.5	22.3	23.0	23.8	24.5	25.3	26.0	26.7	27.5	28.2	29.0	29.7	30.5	31.2	31.9	32.7	33.4	34.2	34.9	35.7	36.4	37.1	37.9	38.6	39.4	40.1	40.9	41.6	42.3	43.1	35
36	17.3	18.1	18.8	19.5	20.2	20.9	21.7	22.4	23.1	23.8	24.6	25.3	26.0	26.7	27.4	28.2	28.9	29.6	30.3	31.1	31.8	32.5	33.2	33.9	34.7	35.4	36.1	36.8	37.6	38.3	39.0	39.7	40.4	41.2	41.9	36
37	16.9	17.6	18.3	19.0	19.7	20.4	21.1	21.8	22.5	23.2	23.9	24.6	25.3	26.0	26.7	27.4	28.1	28.8	29.5	30.2	30.9	31.6	32.3	33.0	33.7	34.4	35.1	35.8	36.5	37.2	37.9	38.6	39.4	40.1	40.8	37
38	16.4	17.1	17.8	18.5	19.2	19.8	20.5	21.2	21.9	22.6	23.3	23.9	24.6	25.3	26.0	26.7	27.4	28.1	28.7	29.4	30.1	30.8	31.5	32.2	32.8	33.5	34.2	34.9	35.6	36.3	36.9	37.6	38.3	39.0	39.7	38
	24	25	26	27	28	29	30	31	32	33	34	35	36	37	38	39	40	41	42	43	44	45	46	47	48	49	50	51	52	53	54	55	56	57	58	

Number of teeth on chainring

TYRE CHART

The first figure in the right-hand column gives the tyre width, the second the diameter of the rim it fits. Both are in millimetres.

Commonly Known as	Standard Designation
Road	
26 x 1.25	32-597
26 x 1.375 (650 x35A)	35-590
26 x 1.5 (650 x35B)	35-584
27 x 0.875	23-630
27 x 1	25-630
27 x 1.125	28-630
27 x 1.25	32-630
27 x 1.375	35-630
28 x1.5 (650 x35B)	35-584
650 x 35A (26 x1.375)	35-590
650 x 35B (26 x1.5)	35-584
700 x 19C	19-622
700 x 20C	20-622
700 x 23C	23-622
700 x 25C	25-622
700 x 28C	28-622
700 x 35C	35-622
700 x 35B (28 x1.5)	35-635
Mountain bike	
26 x 1.5	37-559
26 x 1.75	44-559
26 x 2.125	54-559

Index